# HOME PAGES

## LITERACY LINKS FOR BILINGUAL CHILDREN

# HOME PAGES
## LITERACY LINKS FOR BILINGUAL CHILDREN

*Charmian Kenner*

**Trentham Books**

First published in 2000 by Trentham Books Limited

Trentham Books Limited
Westview House
734 London Road
Oakhill
Stoke on Trent
Staffordshire
England ST4 5NP

**British Cataloguing in Publication Data**
A catalogue record for this book is available from the British Library
ISBN 1 85856 212 0 (hb ISBN 1 85856 211 2)

Designed and typeset by Trentham Print Design Ltd., Chester and printed in Great Britain by Bell & Bain Ltd., Glasgow.

# Contents

# Acknowledgements

I would like to thank my son Darío for being a constant bilingual inspiration;

Chris Brumfit for helping me to think through the original research project in the nursery;

Gunther Kress for frequent exchanges of ideas on children's writing;

Helen Williams and Sarah Horrocks for the pleasure of working together, for their dedication to creating multilingual literacy environments in their classrooms, and for reading the manuscript;

Amarjit Kochhar and Tijen Gemikonakli of the Hackney Under Fives Project for the ongoing stimulation provided by their work on early biliteracy and for commenting on the manuscript;

Kate Rex for her interest in how teachers can promote mother tongue literacy and for her comments on the draft;

Gillian Klein for her friendly and supportive approach as my editor;

Phil Polglaze and the Centre for Language in Primary Education for the photographs;

all the academic colleagues and teacher colleagues who have discussed this work with me in seminars and in-service training sessions;

and of course the children and parents who so enthusiastically brought home literacy materials into school and took part in multilingual writing activities – their ideas are the mainspring of this book.

*For Chris Brumfit,*
*my research supervisor,*
*with thanks and appreciation*

# Introduction

One afternoon, I go into the local hardware store to buy some matches. Simran, the 4 year old daughter of the owners, is playing there happily. She is crouched on the floor, sorting plastic flowerpots into rows in a box. I have seen her in the shop many times since she was a baby. Her father and mother are busy serving other customers, so I ask Simran 'Have you got any matches?'

Immediately she stands up and points to one of the higher shelves. I can't see any matches, so eventually I ask her mother, who laughs and translates 'matches' into Gujarati for Simran. Eagerly, Simran rushes to fetch them for me. She knows exactly where they are kept, behind the counter, because she has sat there many times to watch what was going on in the shop. Now she goes to sit at the till and confidently holds her hand out for the coins I offer her. She takes some change out of the till to give back to me and her father helps her to identify the different coins.

Next Simran hands me a small advertising card, the size and shape of a credit card, and points to the credit card machine. Her father is amused and says that she has often seen him doing credit card transactions. Her mother tells me that Simran watches her sign cheques and wants to write her own name, and indeed as I stand there Simran asks for paper and starts to write boldly across it as if writing a signature. She fills the sheet with writing and asks for another.

During all this time Simran is chatting to me constantly in English. She has recently started attending nursery and her parents are surprised to find how fluent she is. They are keen to support her literacy in English, and also in Gujarati. Her mother will soon start teaching her in Gujarati, and her father is very keen for this to happen. He grew up without learning to write in Gujarati and now feels strongly that this was a loss. Both parents are confident that Simran can become bilingual and biliterate and that this will be an advantage to her.

As I leave the shop, I reflect on my encounter with this self-possessed, knowledgeable 4 year old in her home environment. Simran reminds me of the young bilingual children I have known and worked with in primary school. Like their monolingual classmates, they are fascinated by everyday literacy materials in English, from take-away pizza menus to birthday cards and travel brochures. They also have many literacy experiences at home in other languages, ranging from watching world events on satellite TV in Turkish to reading the Bible with a parent in Spanish. If teachers find out about these experiences and develop connections with them in the classroom, they can tap into huge potential for literacy learning in English and in other languages. Literacy materials brought into school by families can be a resource for this work, acting as 'home pages' for children in the classroom.

## Multilingual literacies: a question of recognition

This book draws on many conversations with teachers. In sessions around Britain from south east England to Scotland, I've talked with teachers about my research on bilingual children's knowledge about literacy. Many have given me further examples of the literacy knowledge shown by bilingual children in their classes, or told me that my findings resonate with their own experiences of growing up bilingual. However, other teachers have been less sure: one of the most common questions I've been asked is 'But surely these children you are telling us about are unusual? What about families who have no literacy?' Some members of the audience have expressed conviction that 'non-literate' bilingual families are the norm rather than the exception. This has led us into discussions about why my experience – of parents and children engaged in literate activity in many languages – is so different from some teachers' perceptions.

Returning to Simran, it is possible that her nursery teacher knows about the procedures I witnessed. She may know that Simran has built up a rich understanding of various purposes for literacy and numeracy through her daily observations in the shop. She may know that Simran sees her mother reading magazines and newspapers in Gujarati as well as in English, and writing letters to India. And finally, she may know that Simran's parents have real hopes that their daughter will grow up as a successful biliterate participant in British society. On the other hand, it is possible that Simran's teacher does not know some or all of these things.

Multilingual literacy knowledge tends to be invisible in the English-speaking school world. In the classroom, materials which are familiar to children at home – such as newspapers, calendars, religious texts, airletters, and videos in different languages – are not available for use and comment. Even when teachers make home visits to establish links with pupils' families, it may seem that 'nothing is there'. This may be because rooms have been tidied in preparation for the visit. Or because books, which are often treated with great care and kept on a high shelf or in a closed cupboard for protection, are simply not noticed by the visitor.

If there are calendars and newspapers in the room, the visitor will probably not see these as evidence of literacy. What most teachers are looking out for is shelves full of children's storybooks, because the storybook is the emblem of school literacy. These books are expected to be either wholly or partly in English, since English is the language of school literacy.

Yes – storybooks are important. They are a vital way of helping children to develop narrative style, a wide vocabulary and imaginative ideas. But they are only one part of children's literacy experience and literacy needs. After they complete school, children will also have to understand (and produce) information texts, letters, plans and reports, and many forms of multi-media communication. Yes – English is important. It is the predominant language of this country and the official one. But in their futures, children from Britain will also need to use many other languages in order to study and work with people in Europe and around the world.

So it is vital that, as educators, we nurture a variety of literacy experiences in a variety of languages – and this is what bilingual children already have. Young children see their grandparents reading newspapers in their first language, and ask what the pictures show and 'What's it about?' Children sit beside their parents when letters are being written to family in other countries and say 'Put my name in the letter – tell them about me'. Then they ask for pen and paper to write their own letters too. Children notice their older siblings doing homework from community language classes in a script which is not like English, and ask 'Why does that writing look different?'

Parents will tell us about these daily experiences if they know that we are interested and genuinely consider that this counts as literacy learning. Children will show their knowledge in the classroom if they feel – at a more than superficial level – that the teacher thinks of biliteracy as an integral part of their education. In the eyes of bilingual parents and children, teachers carry power and authority in this society. They can encourage bilingual literacy experience to flourish – or they can leave it to wither away because there is no place for it in a monolingual curriculum.

If you want to help bilingual children to build on their existing knowledge, this book is for you. Drawing on several years of work with teachers and children in a South London primary school, I offer ideas on how to use home literacy materials in the classroom, and give examples of how particular children have responded by writing in English and in other languages.

## Plan of the book

The book is structured in the following way:

☐ The first chapter suggests how teachers can find out more about children's 'literacy worlds' at home and in their local communities.

☐ The second chapter discusses ways of drawing on these 'literacy worlds' to create a multilingual literacy environment in the classroom.

☐ The third chapter shows that a multilingual environment can encourage children to write in English and in other languages, based on the home experiences which they are now able to bring into school. Examples are given from the work of Billy and Recep, who were motivated by writing in Thai and Turkish respectively.

☐ The fourth chapter considers how children begin to learn about different writing systems by linking and comparing the languages they are using in the classroom. Meera's work in Gujarati and English between the ages of four and seven demonstrates ways in which this can happen.

☐ The fifth chapter looks at how children can take advantage of a multilingual classroom environment in order to design texts which contain a rich variety of graphic symbols. Mohammed, for example, produced recipes, catalogue order forms and alphabet posters by using particular combinations of emergent writing, symbols from Arabic and English, visual images and logos.

The conclusion encourages educators to extend opportunities for children to explore multilingual writing at school. Learning about writing is an interactive process for bilingual children; they transfer their knowledge easily between languages. It is the education system which artificially separates one language from another. When given the opportunity, children will make the most of their multilingual experience to develop a creative and flexible understanding of literacy which will give them the best chance of future success.

CHAPTER ONE

# Literacy Worlds: Biliterate Children, Families and Communities

C hildren are keen-eyed observers of the world around them. They quickly note that the action of typing on a computer keyboard produces marks on a screen, along with logos and images which can be made to move and change colour, and sometimes to speak. Each child wants to be the one to press the keys and make these exciting changes happen. Furthermore, producing marks and images on screen can lead to significant outcomes in terms of building relationships with people (getting an e-mail from family on the other side of the world) or obtaining desirable objects (making money appear out of a hole in the wall). Making marks on pieces of paper can have similar effects: a blue airletter form filled with squiggles is put in the postbox and an envelope comes back from Thailand or Nigeria telling of babies born and weddings being celebrated. An order form with ticks and crosses placed in columns leads to the delivery of toys carefully chosen from the pictures in a colourful catalogue.

For bilingual children, these marks and squiggles come in great variety. Their overall visual appearance may differ noticeably when they are associated with English or with another spoken language. Such marks are part of events experienced in different cultural communities: buying fruit and vegetables in a South Asian shop in the local high street, ordering a meal at a restaurant in Chinatown, watching an Indian film video with the family, or attending worship in which readings are made from the sacred book in a temple or mosque. In each case, texts will be designed and used in ways which are specific to that community and that context.

## Literacy practices at home and at school

Shirley Brice Heath (1983) was one of the first researchers to draw attention to the particularities of literacy events in different cultures. Her rich descriptions of 'ways with words' in the everyday life of two rural communities only a few miles apart in the southeastern USA are now well-known and often-quoted. Accounts of a parent emphasising exactness of interpretation when looking at a storybook with a fractious toddler in 'Roadville', or of a group reading and commenting together on the local newspaper out on the porch in 'Trackton', exemplify different kinds of talk around text. Heath identified patterns in the way literacy events were conducted in each community, and linked these patterns with the underlying organisation of social life (such as adult-child relationships, and the moral values which were considered to be important). Such patterns of social activity around reading and writing have been termed 'literacy practices' by Brian Street (1984).

School literacy practices are often alien to those of local communities. In Heath's research, for example, both Trackton and Roadville children encountered difficulties when they began school, since the school ways of using spoken and written language did not fit with those of their communities. Teachers were perplexed by what they saw as children's failure to conform to school norms. Unaware that their pupils indeed had literacy histories – but of another kind – they interpreted lack of response in the classroom as lack of knowledge. Eventually, this vicious circle of misunderstanding doomed Roadville and Trackton children to failure in terms of school literacy.

Eve Gregory (1993) has pointed out that similar misunderstandings occur in Britain today. For example, children of Bangladeshi origin in London's East End tend to be seen as having 'problems' with literacy in their primary school classrooms. Yet many of the same children are enthusiastic literacy learners when observed in their community-run Bengali and Arabic classes. Most primary teachers, however, do not realise that their 6 year old pupils are participating in these out-of-school classes for up to ten hours a week, and are already beginning to read and write in two other languages. They may also not realise that the patterns of interaction around text in community language schools, although quite unlike the teaching methods used in primary schools, can successfully promote learning.

**Crossing the home-school divide**

Why does the gulf between home and school persist? Perhaps because there has traditionally been a built-in expectation on the part of the education system that a certain percentage of children are bound to fail. This expectation may be changing, but even now bilingual children – together with white children from non-middle class backgrounds – are seen as 'outside the mainstream' and therefore as 'lacking in literacy', with school input designed to fill that gap.

When researchers actually observe in homes and ask parents about family reading and writing activities, a very different picture emerges. Denny Taylor (1983) began her research in white middle-class American homes. She documented children's involvement in family literacy, both in routines organised by adults such as the bedtime story and in informal moments set up by children themselves, for example when a 2 year old wrote alone at a desk in the living room. Later, Taylor worked with Cathe Dorsey-Gaines (1988) to conduct similar research with black families living in urban poverty in New York City. There she also found parents and children engaged in a range of literacy activities, from helping with homework to writing letters and decoding official forms from Government institutions. Parents devoted time and energy to literacy as part of everyday life, and were eager for their children to succeed, yet the researchers observed these children being stereotyped and ignored in classrooms.

Taylor and Dorsey-Gaines advocated that educators should get to know their pupils' literacy strengths and build on them. Everyday literacy can very effectively be brought into classroom work, as Nigel Hall and Anne Robinson have demonstrated in Britain (1995). They describe how children in a primary school class made their home corner into a 'garage', and how this provided numerous writing opportunities. Inspired by a visit to a local garage, the 5 year olds produced safety instructions for welding, job applications to become a mechanic, and invitations to the 'grand opening' of their garage. As part of the process of building the garage, children also filled in real planning application forms from the Town Hall, and were carefully led by the teacher through the stages of devising a formal letter in response to an objection which was sent in by one of the researchers in the guise of 'a local resident'. Thus by the end of the project these young children had developed a wide range of texts, all of which relate to literacy requirements specified in the National Curriculum.

**3**

## Multilingual literacies

I have just described how teachers can use everyday literacy in English as a resource for learning. What is known about children's literacy experience in other languages, and how it can be brought into the classroom? Apart from the work of Eve Gregory and her colleagues Nasima Rashid and Ann Williams (see Rashid and Gregory, 1997), which highlighted the role of community language schools, young bilingual children's home literacy environments in Britain have been little-researched. The evidence which we do have so far, however, is exciting in its scope.

As part of his discussion on the complex multilingual reading and writing abilities of Panjabi families in Southall, West London, Mukul Saxena (1994) describes the typical day of a 4 year old. This boy observes his parents and grandparents reading newspapers and novels, and writing letters and shopping lists, in Panjabi, Hindi and English. As a result, he can distinguish between three different types of script, although his school literacy experience is restricted to English only. Research with older children and young people aged 9–20 in the Gujarati-speaking community in Leicester, by Marilyn Martin-Jones and Arvind Bhatt (1999), shows them adding their news to fortnightly family letters written to relatives abroad, joining in with prayer gatherings at home, reading novels and performing songs in Gujarati. Again, there is no opportunity for them to extend these literacies in their mainstream school environment – but if children from age 4 upwards were encouraged to do so, this could bring rich rewards in terms of literacy learning.

## Finding out about literacies in a nursery class

It was with the awareness that young bilingual children are likely to have such varied experiences that I began the research project which I shall describe in this book. I worked collaboratively with Helen, the teacher in a South London nursery class, for a full school year, during which we aimed to develop a multilingual literacy environment in the classroom. Our purpose was to find out about the literacy knowledge which children were acquiring at home, and to encourage writing at school in other languages as well as English. This approach stimulated a great deal of writing during the year, both from bilingual children and from their monolingual classmates.

First, Helen and I needed to get to know the bilingual children and parents in the nursery in a new kind of way. We were interested in their 'literacy worlds' at home and in local communities. The process of learning about these worlds took some time. We began chatting with parents when they came into the classroom in the morning and afternoon, asking about any materials in different languages which their children liked to use at home, and encouraging them to bring these into the nursery. We ourselves brought in newspapers, magazines and alphabet learning books in different languages which we had been given or found in local shops, and asked parents for comments. We observed children's reactions to these multilingual materials in the nursery and listened to their talk with their classmates.

After the project had been underway for several weeks, the time felt right for me to ask parents if they could spare a few minutes for an informal interview. The 'few minutes' turned into half an hour or longer, with parents sitting at the nursery's writing table or in the small waiting area, often with children coming up and adding their own remarks. As well as asking about reading and writing activities at home, I was able to show parents some of the 'everyday' writing the children had done in the home corner at the nursery, such as cafe menus and greeting cards. Parents then realised that I was interested in this kind of material and not merely trying to find out whether home ex-

4

periences replicated 'official' school literacy. They relaxed and began to chat about the 'pizza delivery' games played at home, or the way their children joined in with writing birthday cards.

## Literacy worlds

I shall now describe the 'literacy worlds' of the children you will meet in this book, based on the information which we gathered from these experiences. This information is inevitably restricted – no more than a partial window onto a highly complex world. If I, as the researcher, could have spent months observing events in homes and accompanying families everywhere from video shops to temples, I would have learnt a great deal more. As it was, my role as a researcher in the classroom required me to concentrate my energies, with the teacher, on building a multilingual environment in the nursery. However, this means that our access to knowledge about children's literacy environments, gained through conversations with parents at school and through listening to children, was not very different from that which is potentially available to any classroom teacher. Over time, parents will respond to a consistent interest in their children's bilingual experience, and an ongoing dialogue about multilingual literacy can grow within the classroom. Teachers will gradually be able to build a picture of children's wider literacy knowledge and understand how it stems from everyday social and cultural life.

5

I have used diagrams to represent the children's literacy worlds. These are a way of representing the multi-layered language and literacy environments in which bilingual children live. Each layer represents an area of experience, a 'domain', such as home or school. I have arranged these layers to show how each domain was located with respect to the child – so 'home' is the most central, with 'Thailand' or 'India' being the furthest away. I have also tried to indicate the significance of each domain in terms of the amount of time the child spent there – thus 'school' is placed between 'home' and 'local community'. I have noted some of the people with whom the child communicated in each language, and some important places where literacy events might happen. I have also mentioned particular texts in languages other than English which were part of the children's lives.

The 'school' layer involved parents and children bringing texts in different languages from home into school, and using them together as a resource for writing in the classroom. The aim was to bring the literacy materials familiar to children from the 'home' domain into the 'school' domain. This will be discussed in detail in the next chapter.

The languages mentioned are the predominant ones used with each person or in a particular place. The children and the bilingual people around them would be switching between their first languages and English as a matter of course in most settings. Also, many texts the children encountered would contain more than one language; for example, newspapers produced for bilingual communities in Britain include articles in English and advertisements in both languages. These are complex issues and the diagrams operate only as a rough guide to remind us of the variety of children's literacy experience and the many possible areas in which they can participate.

## Billy's literacy world (see Fig.1)

Billy was 3 years 5 months old in the autumn term when the research began. His mother spoke Thai and his father English, and he had a baby sister, Elizabeth. When Billy and his sister were together with their mother, she spoke to them mainly in Thai; Billy spoke English with his father.

Billy's mother was teaching him the alphabet in both Thai and English. To help with Thai, he had a colourful alphabet book in which each letter was illustrated with a picture. His mother lent this book to us for reference in the classroom writing area. When Billy and I looked at the book together, Billy told me that his mum had brought it to school and he confirmed that she wrote like the writing inside.

Billy would also sit next to his mother at home when she wrote letters to the family in Thailand. He would say to her 'write you, Billy, Elizabeth', because he wanted all these names to be included in the letter. Meanwhile, he would write on his own sheets of paper, doing various symbols or 'wavy-line' writing.

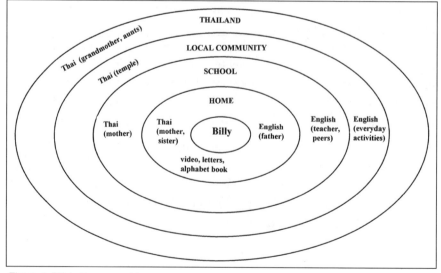

*Figure 1: Billy's literacy world*

6

Billy's favourite literacy item in Thai, according to his mother, was a karaoke video. This showed romantic songs performed amongst beautiful river scenery, with the Thai script rippling across the screen in time with the singer's voice. Billy's mother told me which songs he particularly enjoyed, and we watched these in the nursery. Billy introduced the video confidently in English, explaining that it would show boats and fishing.

Billy also enjoyed videos and cartoons in English at home. Other literacy items which interested him were pictures of famous football players – he was beginning to recognise some of them and could say the names of several teams – and signs for fast food restaurants on the street.

Although Billy did not have access to a large community of Thai speakers locally, and his experiences outside the home were therefore mainly in English, his mother sometimes took him to the Thai temple in another part of London. When they visited the temple, Billy would say 'Mu-ang Thai' ('Thailand'). He may also have been referring to the Thai script which he would have seen in the building.

Billy knew that his grandmother and aunts lived in Thailand; when looking at family photos which his mother had brought to the nursery, he said 'Mu-ang Thai'. He made the same comments about some pages which he and his mother had produced about Thailand for a 'travel brochure' in the nursery.

7

Even at the age of 3, Billy was therefore learning about writing in more than one language and script, and his literacy world extended as far as Thailand. Some of his writing activities were structured, such as the alphabet sessions with his mother. At other times he participated informally, such as in letter writing, when he sensed the importance of communicating with the family he knew only through photos.

## Meera's literacy world (see Fig.2)

Meera was 3 years 10 months old when the project began. Her mother and father were Gujarati speakers, and she had a 9 year old sister, Pinal. Both Pinal and Meera had been born and brought up in London.

At home, Meera heard her parents speaking to each other in Gujarati, and this was also the language they used mainly with the children. Pinal had already spent several years in school, and so she played with Meera in English as well as in Gujarati. Comments by Meera in the nursery showed that she was aware of these differences. She told me that her mum 'speaks Gujarati', her dad 'says in Gujarati', whilst her sister 'speaks Gujarati' and also 'can't talk Gujarati'.

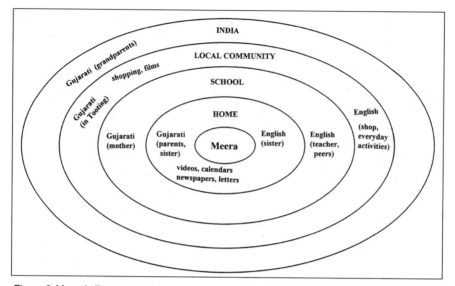

*Figure 2: Meera's literacy world*

Meera was being taught to write in English at home, but not yet in Gujarati, since her parents thought it would be too difficult for her to learn both scripts at once. However, her father told me how he encouraged her writing in general, suggesting for example that she copied into an exercise book from newspapers, books or any other material to hand. Since some of these materials were in Gujarati, Meera would try out both scripts. She would refer to a Gujarati magazine, saying 'I'm writing it', and her mother would respond 'You can try'.

Meera demonstrated her knowledge about home literacy materials as soon as the multilingual work began in the nursery. When her mother first wrote in Gujarati in the classroom, Meera began to talk about 'films' and 'TV' – she was referring to the Indian films which the family watched on video. Meera brought her favourite video to school and we watched several excerpts; the title on the label was in Gujarati.

Meera and her mother also brought in calendars which they used at home. One of these was a Hindu religious calendar. Meera understood its significance and its use; she told me the pictures included 'Bhagwan', and commented that 'numbers are in it'. Another was a calendar in Gujarati, which she said was kept 'on the wall above the heater' at home. She identified some of the writing in it as Gujarati, and showed that she knew the purpose of the numbers when she asked 'Do you know when is my birthday? Eleven – my mummy says eleven' (her birthday was on the eleventh of the month).

Meera's mother read several Gujarati newspapers at home. Meera recognised a copy of one of these when it was being used in the nursery, carrying it round with her and saying 'mummy mummy mummy!' On another occasion, she found the newspaper in my bag and said 'read to my mum'.

As in Billy's family, letter-writing to relatives abroad was an important activity. When her mother wrote the family airletters to India in Gujarati, Meera was a keen participant. She sat alongside her mother, saying 'I'm writing a letter' and doing her own 'wavy-line' writing.

Meanwhile, Meera was also involved in informal writing in English when playing with her sister. 'School' was a favourite theme, with Meera liking to assign roles by saying 'You are Sharon (the nursery nurse), I am Helen (the teacher)'. Meera would give verbal instructions that she had heard at nursery, and the games would include writing. One morning Meera came into school flourishing a large brown envelope with a 'register' of the nursery children's names on, apparently written by her sister. Children were marked present or absent, and the envelope was completely covered with additional writing, including a noughts and crosses game.

Meera's literacy experience outside her immediate home environment also involved both Gujarati and English. She often mentioned that her family went shopping in Tooting, a nearby area where there was a large South Asian community. She told me, for example, that her mother went to the 'film shop' there. With labels on the fruit and vegetables for sale, posters in shop windows, and the associated talk with shopkeepers and friends, this local area would have been a key domain for Meera's understanding of Gujarati.

The family ran a small local supermarket not far from the school. They lived above the shop and Meera spent a good deal of time there. Here she would see and hear mostly English. She was fascinated by the leaflets, coupons and stickers in the shop, often bringing these into the nursery. Meera's mother described how her older daughter Pinal would play at filling in delivery and order forms in the shop, and was learning to take orders over the phone. Meera would copy her sister in roleplay at home.

Finally, Meera's grandparents lived in Gujarat, in north-west India. As well as being involved in writing letters on airmail paper which were posted to India, Meera also knew that she would soon be visiting India for the first time. Like Billy, her domains of literacy were many, varied and far-reaching.

### Mohammed's literacy world (see Fig.3)

Mohammed was 4 years 8 months old when the research began. His parents had come to Britain from the Gujarati-speaking community in Malawi, East Africa. Mohammed was the youngest in the family, with an older brother aged 12 and a sister aged 10. The family spoke Gujarati as well as English at home, and since they were Muslim, Arabic was also important as a religious language.

Mohammed's sister, Shaista, would write the English alphabet out for him and he would copy from this, so he could now write the letters A-G and his name, along with the numbers 1-15. As well as encouraging him to write in English at home, Mohammed's mother was teaching him to read Arabic letters – using an alphabet chart and song tape – so that he would be ready to go to Qur'anic classes. Shaista already attended these community-run courses after school for two hours a day, five days a week, and Mohammed would begin at age 5. Everyone in the family apart from Mohammed had their own copy of the Qur'an, which they treated with care and respect. Mohammed would receive his copy when he had reached the required level of reading in Arabic.

According to his mother, Mohammed was a keen participant in home literacy activities; he was 'always asking for pen and paper'. When she wrote letters to relatives in Gujarati, Mohammed sat beside her, adding his own 'wavy-line' writing on the same page. He would ask her 'What have you written? Read it to me', and he commented that the script looked different. He would write letters to his older cousin, who lived nearby, and pin her replies up on his wall. He would also make texts about his favourite subject, his father's car, saying for example 'This is Daddy changing the wheel'.

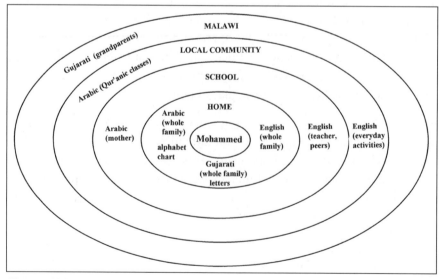

*Figure 3: Mohammed's literacy world*

Mohammed engaged in many play activities at home involving literacy. His mother had made him a toy corner which he would turn into a shop, a cafe or a garage. He would sally forth from his 'Burgerking shop' pretending to deliver pizzas on a motorbike, instructing his mother to 'Phone me and tell me what you want'. With his miniature Matchbox school set, he would become the teacher, with his toys as the pupils. He asked his mother to draw up a register in an old register book brought from school.

Mohammed knew of the Qur'anic classes his sister attended in the local community. When out on the street, he would ask his mother questions about the signs he saw in English, and try to read them out. He could also discriminate between different makes of vehicle, since cars were his special interest, and could recognise names such as 'Vauxhall'.

Further afield, Mohammed was aware that his grandparents lived in another country. Again, this was emphasised by the letter-writing activity in Gujarati.

These then were the literacy worlds of Billy, Meera and Mohammed – seen through our small window of knowledge built up in the nursery. As we worked with children and parents throughout the year, our pictures of their literacy experience became more vivid and extensive. When we made use of multilingual materials brought from home into the classroom, parents and children gained confidence, leading them to tell us more. Thus there was an interaction between our understanding of children's literacy worlds and the participation of parents and children in multilingual activities at school. This participation is described and discussed in the next chapter.

11

### Ideas for finding out about home literacy

Below are suggestions which arise from the research I have discussed in this chapter. If you are working in partnership with bilingual assistants, their expertise and knowledge about local communities will be of great help in all these areas.

- As teachers know, nursery and reception classes are the ideal time to establish relationships with parents (and with grandparents, siblings and other family members). It's crucial that they feel welcome in the class-room and can chat informally with staff about their children's needs and interests.

- For bilingual families, the welcome needs to include an appreciation of the languages they speak, read and write. Multilingual 'Welcome' posters at the door are an important first step. But the posters remain a token presence unless the dialogue goes further.

- In conversations with parents and other family members, teachers can show interest in bilingual literacy activities which may happen at home.

You could ask 'Do you read or write anything in another language? Does your child see you doing this or do it with you? Are there any videos/ tapes/books/TV stations/magazines which they like looking at and listening to?' (Audiovisual materials may be particularly popular – for instance, families may watch first language stations on satellite TV).

- You can underline your interest by inviting parents to bring home literacy materials into the classroom. Your enthusiasm for finding out what children do at home will encourage families to do this.

- You may need to start the ball rolling by bringing in texts in different languages. Newspapers, magazines, alphabet teaching materials, and film and video posters are excellent conversation-starters. These can be found in bookshops or video and music shops run by different ethnic communities. Shopkeepers will help you to gather materials, particularly if you mention that you are going to use them with children at school.

- Parents may at first seem to speak little English when talking with the teachers, but this may be because they feel nervous and tongue-tied. Bilingual literacy materials can act as an ice-breaker for communication. Parents can indicate, by gesture as well as talk, whether they use these and when, and whether their children like them. Older siblings in the school who are confident speakers of English can visit your classroom and comment too.

- Parent-teacher conferences are a key moment to confirm your interest in children's bilingual learning. What is discussed and recorded at these meetings carries the official sanction of 'school literacy'. It's important to include questions about home literacy (e.g. as part of filling in the Primary Language Record). If you have some examples such as bilingual newspapers with you, this will show that you have a wide view of what 'literacy' means.

- Children themselves will often want to comment on what they do with home literacy materials. Some may speak confidently alongside their parents. Once the materials are in the classroom, you can also keep an ear open for children's remarks to each other, when you pass the home corner, reading corner or writing area.

- Finding out about home literacy can take time – time for parents to trust you and believe that your interest in bilingualism is more than a token, time for them to realise that you are not only checking whether they read the right kinds of books to their children. If the dialogue builds up, it will open out new worlds of understanding between school and home, and be a rich and rewarding part of your relationship with parents and children.

CHAPTER TWO

# Making the Links: Building on Home Literacy Experience in School

When bilingual children enter primary school, their literacy worlds often narrow to one language only. My own involvement with multilingual work in school began from this perception. My son had attended a Latin American nursery until age 4, where his learning had been nurtured in Spanish by teacher-carers called 'tías' and 'tíos' ('aunts' and 'uncles') who acted as an extended family. When children 'graduated' from the nursery, they were regarded as part of its community for life, with their photos displayed on the nursery walls as 'ex-alumnos', and a standing invitation to events in the nursery calendar. Yet there was little place for my son's hugely significant early learning experiences in Spanish when he reached primary school. English was the only language in use. In that sense, school felt like a language-deprived environment.

Like my son, many children have received their early literacy education in mother-tongue nurseries. Even more children have learnt about reading and writing in different languages informally in homes and communities, as described in the previous chapter. How can schools build on this knowledge rather than excluding it?

## Bilingualism as a resource for learning

The National Literacy Strategy's framework for teaching recognises the potential for children to make use of first language knowledge when learning to read and write in English. The framework suggests that children can draw on their awareness of the principles of spelling and phonology to help them understand the English writing system. Also, 'talking about literacy in languages other than English can help...to identify points of similarity and difference between languages at word, sentence and text level' (1998, p.107).

These suggestions fit well with research on bilingual learning. The way that knowledge can be transferred between languages has been discussed by Jim Cummins (1984, 1991). He shows how concepts and ideas developed in one language can interact with those developed in another, because the thinking involved is going on at a deeper level. It's as though what we see of children's language use is only the tip of the iceberg – two tips in the case of bilingual children, so it's a double iceberg – with most of their ideas about how languages work being generated in the strong unifying base of the double iceberg, an invisible area which lies below the surface of the water.

The metaphor of the 'double iceberg' is taken up by Colin Baker in his parents' and teachers' guide to bilingualism (1995). With regard to literacy, he explains that children transfer reading and writing skills from one language to another. Once they understand that letters can stand for sounds, or that words can be guessed from the storyline, these general principles can be applied elsewhere.

Cummins' theory is supported by many research studies (such as those described in Baker, 1996, Chapter 8) which have found that bilingual children, because of their experience of dealing with more than one language, notice the way different language systems operate. This 'metalinguistic awareness' gives them the ability to analyse and manipulate language in ways which monolingual children tend not to do. Eve Gregory (1996) explains how bilingual children use this awareness to call upon 'clues' about pronunciation, vocabulary and grammar when learning to read in another language. If teachers understand what is happening, they can support children's strategies.

**14**

So bilingualism can be an aid to children's learning. In the United States, where bilingual education programmes have been under way for some time, mostly in Spanish and English, there is convincing evidence that children who learn in both languages actually do better than monolingual children in the long term. This is particularly obvious in programmes called 'two-way bilingual education', where all children – whether they are from Spanish-speaking families or from monolingual English backgrounds – learn in both languages throughout their school career. These young people gained higher results in English than the national average by the end of secondary school (Thomas and Collier, 1997). Another study found that primary school children's learning of English and maths was enhanced if they had been taught partly in their mother tongue, Spanish, up to Year 6 (Ramirez, 1992).

But in England there are no bilingual programmes in state education. The National Literacy Strategy advice I mentioned is given in one paragraph only, headed 'The place of languages other than English'. All the advice is directed towards the learning of English, and pupils are referred to as having 'English as an additional language' rather than as 'children who are becoming biliterate'. This implies that 'the place of other languages' is marginal. The only reason for using them in the classroom is for extra help in acquiring the school language, English.

## Biliteracy as a resource for the future

Is it wise to pay so little attention to biliteracy? In the future, all children are likely to need more bilingual experience rather than less. A recent European Commission report on education and training (1996) predicts that children will need to be confident users of at least three languages in order to take advantage of the study and job opportunities available to them in Europe in the future. The report recommends that children should learn other languages from pre-school onwards. This is an urgent issue for British policymakers to take on. In the meantime, many children in Britain come to pre-school and primary school with knowledge already of another language, and would be well equipped to acquire further languages through their bilingual ex-perience. Schools need to do as much as they can to support bilingual chil-dren – their knowledge is both an individual resource and a national treasure.

This is the attitude taken by the Welsh Language Board in promoting Welsh-English bilingualism in education, from pre-school through primary and secondary schooling. The Board produces leaflets for parents, and for health and education professionals, with titles such as *Two Languages: Twice the Choice* (1999). These explain the advantages of bilingualism, including:

– more creative and flexible thinking
– increased curricular achievement
– ease in learning a third language
– twice the enjoyment of reading and writing
– access to two cultures and worlds of experience
– enhanced economic and employment benefits.

**15**

The same advantages apply to bilingualism in other languages. But if the education system ignores languages other than English, children may not be able to make the most of their bilingual experience. The Welsh Language Board points out that Welsh children used to be denied the chance to speak Welsh in school and were looked down upon for being bilingual. Now that is changing. Bilingual education is giving children a positive sense of self-esteem and confidence, a feeling of security in their linguistic and cultural identity.

The issue of self-esteem is particularly important for children whose lan-guage background differs from that of the mainstream. Jim Cummins (1996) shows that when bilingual children can work with their teachers to build up a strong cultural identity in the classroom, this promotes their academic development. Being able to use their home languages is a key part of the process; language and identity are strongly linked.

## Supporting bilingual learning

So how could bilingual learning be encouraged throughout Britain? In some schools, many children share a language, so bilingual education could be a feasible option. In others, children come from a huge variety of backgrounds, or there may be very few bilingual children in the school. In all cases, the first step is for schools to have a language policy which explicitly states that bilingual learning is considered important and will be supported wherever possible. A national language policy of this kind is also needed, along with multilingual learning opportunities being built into the National Curriculum. Maggie Gravelle (1996) discusses these issues and suggests ways of formulat-

onder how they can support a variety of languages in their classroom when they speak few or none of them. There is help at hand! The experience of educators who have successfully encouraged multilingual learning in schools is available. Examples of classroom practice are gathered together in a number of publications, including those by David Houlton (1985), the National Writing Project (1990) and Viv Edwards (1998). The Multilingual Resources for Children Project (1995) investigates a range of resources in different languages, and considers how bilingual texts can be given a high status in a school environment.

16 All of these publications demonstrate the importance of children being able to actively use their first languages in classroom work. Many schools want to show that they value bilingualism, and for this reason they display 'welcome' posters in different languages, ask parents to help with translating labels for the classroom, and include dual-language books in the reading corner. These are indeed necessary first steps in creating a multilingual ethos. But there is a big difference between simply displaying other languages in the classroom and actually encouraging children to engage with multilingual writing in their daily literacy activities. When the writing comes off the wall and is transformed into children's own texts, it comes alive and gains a clear purpose. The strongest way schools can show their support for bilingualism is by making it part of learning.

## Home literacy materials in the classroom

The project described in this book complements other work on bilingual learning, by focusing specifically on how to promote the use of home texts in school. By 'home texts' I mean literacy materials which are familiar to children from their everyday experience – the calendar which hung on Meera's wall, the alphabet chart which Mohammed used with his mother. These will carry different meanings for children from the multilingual materials produced by the school. Translations of classroom labels and dual-language books have their own important uses. But they come from the angle of the school – translations are requested from parents for school purposes, dual-language books are based on the school storybook model. It is rare for children to use materials which are actually part of their home environment at school, yet there is so much potential here for connecting with the excitement and interest which comes from participating in family literacy events.

## Creating a multilingual literacy environment

These are the connections which the teacher and I wanted to make in the South London nursery class. Setting up a multilingual literacy environment was part of our general aim of bringing home literacy into school, in both English and other languages. Everyday literacy materials in English were of course easily available, and we placed a good many in the home corner, such as magazines, catalogues, telephone directories and calendars. We also provided a tray full of writing materials: different sizes of paper, old forms from the school office, message pads, envelopes and pens. Children could play and write in the home corner, and also in the writing area which had a large table next to shelves well stocked with a similar range of resources. We kept up a dialogue with all the parents about their children's literacy interests at home, and showed them the writing produced by the children in the nursery.

**17**

We particularly needed the help of bilingual parents to provide materials from home in different languages, and to explain their children's 'literacy worlds' to us. The families whose children came to the nursery spoke many different languages, including Arabic, Cantonese, Gujarati, Filipino, Spanish, Thai, Tigrinya and Yoruba. By talking with parents in the ways described in the last chapter, we began to discover that some were already teaching their children to write in their home language as well as English. When we asked if there were any materials that children particularly enjoyed looking at and using in home languages, we received a whole variety of answers, ranging from alphabet materials to airletters and videos.

We encouraged families to bring items into the nursery, and these were some examples:

- Mohammed and his mother brought an audiotape of the Arabic alphabet song which she was using to prepare Mohammed for Qur'anic classes. Mohammed enjoyed listening to the children's voices as they sang the names of the alphabet letters. His mother also brought a set of flashcards which accompanied the song, and a small chart showing the Qur'anic alphabet.

- Marta and her father brought one of the videos which Marta particularly liked to watch at home: it was a recording of a fundraising concert for Eritrea which took place in Italy. The video showed songs being performed in Tigrinya to a huge audience in a football stadium. Banners could be seen on the concert platform in Tigrinya and Arabic.

- Danny and his mother brought a Spanish storybook of 'The Lion King', the current Disney film favourite around the world. The book was a present to Danny from his uncle in Ecuador, and it was accompanied by an audiotape of the story, which Danny knew by heart.

- Meera and her mother brought Meera's favourite Indian film video, 'Nashib'. This included many lively singing and dancing sequences which Meera loved. The film was in Hindi, with the title being written on the video label in Meera's home language, Gujarati.

- Meera and her mother also brought two calendars from home. One was a Hindu calendar, with an illustration of a religious scene for each month. The captions for each picture were in English, and the numbers were Arabic numerals as used in Britain. The other was in Gujarati with Gujarati numerals.

- Billy and his mother brought his favourite item in Thai – the karaoke video. The background to the romantic interaction between the singers was a wide river with lush vegetation, on which fishing boats plied their trade. The Thai script accompanying the songs was prominent on the screen.

*Sharing literacy materials brought from home*

Bringing these materials to the nursery was a source of pride for the children. The videos, books, tapes and calendars were familiar objects from their home life, which were now present in school and were seen as important by their teacher and friends. When the materials were used in class, children responded with enthusiasm and confidence. Billy, who was usually hesitant about talking in front of a group, stood up and spoke with unexpected fluency in English when he introduced his karaoke video to the whole class. Marta showed her pleasure when the Eritrean video was shown, by bouncing and swaying to the music. Danny led small groups in listening to his 'Lion King' tape and reading the accompanying storybook, announcing his favourite phrases resonantly in Spanish and showing other children when to turn the page. He then performed the song from the tape for the whole class with considerable panache.

## Parents as writers

As well as welcoming home literacy materials into the nursery, we invited parents and other family members to act as writers in the classroom. As an initial activity to signal a welcome for multilingual writing, several parents sat together in the nursery's writing area to translate parts of a display called 'Our Nursery Rules', which had been made by the teacher and children at the beginning of the school year. Each bilingual child chose a rule which they would like their parent to translate. From this school-based text we moved on to activities which connected with literacy experience at home. For example, Ace's mother, who was teaching her daughter to write Chinese numbers at home, came into the nursery to write numbers with a small group of children. Adedamola's mother and Meera's mother helped their children to write cards, in Yoruba and Gujarati respectively, for the class 'postbox'. Billy's mother, Marta's father, and Meera's mother sat at the nursery's writing table and showed how they wrote airletters to family abroad.

19

When parents wrote in the nursery, their children often did their own writing at the same time or shortly afterwards. Sitting with pen in hand, alongside an adult who was an important role model, gave children the chance to participate in the act of 'being a writer'. When Billy talked about a symbol he produced after seeing his mother write an airletter in Thai, he said 'I write like my mum'. When adding to a text produced by her mother, Meera said 'I write Gujarati. I write like my mum'.

Parental writing held a special status for these young children, and could have an inspirational effect. Adedamola watched his mother write in Yoruba and immediately made marks on her text, using the same colours. A month later, he copied some of the words she had written, paying great attention to the form of the letters and their sequence. Since Adedamola usually only

*Mother and daughter writing together in the classroom*

*Talking about Gujarati writing*

produced one or two letters of his name at this stage, his response demonstrated the motivating power of his mother's writing.

Since home language use was strongly connected with their families and rarely encountered in school, seeing their parents participate as writers in the classroom was a significant event for bilingual children. Meera highlighted its importance when she informed me on one occasion: 'my mum writing in the nursery', and repeated the same words to nursery staff later that day. Children appreciated having their parents' writing continually present in the nursery and being able to interact with it. Ace put this into words as she added a photograph to her mother's writing of the words 'Hong Kong' in Chinese, saying 'I want to put it next to my mummy's writing' and 'I like my mummy's writing'.

## The teacher's role

The messages put across by Helen, the teacher, to parents and children were a key element in the success of the nursery as a multilingual environment. Helen felt that work in different languages would be educationally beneficial to all the children in the nursery and she had made a positive decision to encourage multilingualism as part of classroom life. Throughout the year, she created a welcoming atmosphere for parents as writers and was ready to make the most of children's bilingual writing whenever it occurred – both at expected and unexpected moments.

**21**

Helen gave particular space to discussion of children's work when the whole nursery class was assembled together, sitting on the carpet in the book corner. At this time, she would invite children to show their home literacy materials and the writing they had done. Helen would then discuss the multilingual texts with the whole class, encouraging children to compare and comment on the way writing was used in different languages. Monolingual children were involved in writing and commenting too, as will be seen from the examples below. Discussion also went on in small groups and with individuals when the multilingual writing activities were taking place in the classroom.

## The children's participation

We treated the children as emergent bilingual writers, who often had more knowledge of their home language than we did ourselves. Even though these children were very young, 3 and 4 years old, they had comments to make based on their keen observations of family and community literacy practices. The presence of home texts in the nursery, and the activities based around them, made it possible for children to contribute their knowledge when talking with classmates and staff.

The multilingual literacy environment was thus an interactive and flexible one, in which children could develop their own agendas. They could refer back to parental writing and home texts throughout the school day. These materials were available in the home corner or the writing area, or could be taken down from displays on the classroom walls whenever children wished to look at them. Children could also display their own writing on the home corner walls, and take it down and add to it when they wanted to.

The children understood the routines of the nursery well and knew that the home corner was a place where they could particularly develop spontaneous writing and display their texts. They were keen for an adult to participate in their role-plays and help them with writing, and would often approach me saying 'Let's go to the home corner'. Meera, for example, enjoyed displaying her work there and one day she commented about some Gujarati alphabet sheets 'That's nice – can you see that, put it in the home corner?' She also explicitly showed her awareness that multilingual work was welcomed at 'group time' by asking me several times 'Can I show it on carpet?' when she finished a piece of writing. Monolingual children also recognised that multi-lingual activities were part of nursery life. Michaela, sitting with me at the writing table, wrote a text which she said was Chinese and English, and added 'Shall I do some more Chinese? We always do Chinese on this table'.

**22**

*Writng her own Gujarati*

## Home texts as part of the curriculum

It was vital to ensure that home texts became an integral part of children's work in the nursery. This would give multilingual literacy materials high status, and children would be able to use them for learning at school as well as at home. As families told us about home literacy events and brought materials into the nursery, the teacher and I devised ways of building on this input in classroom activities. Below I describe several of the ways in which we did so.

## Learning about letters and numbers

Alphabet and number work in the nursery could draw on other languages as a resource. When Mohammed and his mother brought in the tape of an Arabic alphabet song and the accompanying flashcards, Mohammed began by showing the cards to a small group of classmates and identifying some of the letters he knew. Helen and I then planned to listen to the tape with the whole nursery group and sing along with the song. Since we did not know the names of the letters, we asked Mohammed's mother if she could make a poster based on the alphabet chart which they used at home, with a trans-literation of the sound of each letter for us to read as we sang. A few days later Mohammed and his mother brought this home-made poster (overleaf) to school, and the whole class sang the alphabet together while I pointed to each letter.

**23**

The Arabic tape was available for children to put into the cassette player themselves and listen to at other moments in the nursery day. They also enjoyed a lively 'Rock ABC' song on cassette, and I made a large poster of the English alphabet to go with it. The English and Arabic alphabet posters were on the nursery wall, next to each other. One day I found Adedamola, Adedayo, Colin and Stefanie dancing to the 'Rock ABC' tape and pointing to different letters on the Arabic poster. The following week this happened again. On another occasion, Megan pointed to the Arabic poster whilst singing 'A B C D'.

The experience of different written alphabets accompanying different songs had reinforced the idea that spoken language is represented by written symbols. This is an important understanding in early literacy learning. Mohammed, because of his home experience, could already identify which song related to which poster. When I saw him looking at the Arabic tape box and asked him 'Do you know which song it is?', he nodded and pointed to the Arabic poster. I also saw him copying the alphabet from his mother's poster while singing the song to himself.

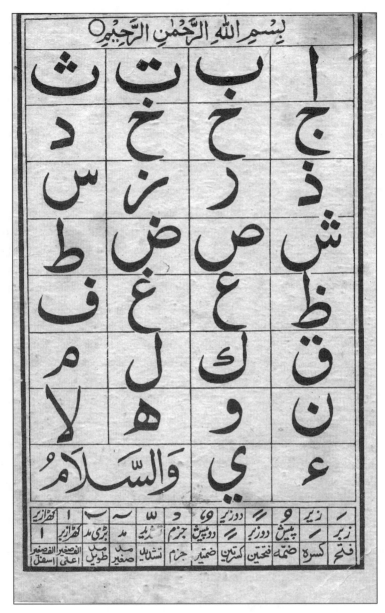

Figure 4: Mohammed's Arabic alphabet chart

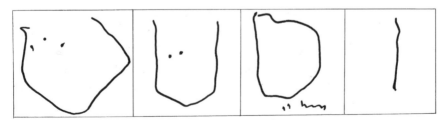

Figure 5: Vanessa's writing of Arabic alphabet letters.
After the first letter (from right to left) comes 'shoe, two shoes, three shoes'

24

Children made their own alphabet posters, with the Arabic and English ones as examples. Vanessa, sitting alongside Mohammed, wrote the first few letters of the Arabic alphabet, from right to left. These include three symbols which look like upturned semi-circles – the first has a dot underneath, the second and third have two dots and three dots inside them respectively. As she wrote them, Vanessa said 'shoe', 'two shoes', and 'three shoes' (see Figs. 4 and 5). The semi-circles could be perceived by a child as shoes, and Vanessa was also bringing her knowledge of the number system to bear on her writing. Her actions illustrate how children will make use of the symbols present in their literacy environment to explore how writing operates.

Numbers were of considerable interest to the children. When Ace's mother came into the classroom to write Chinese numbers, and when we looked at Meera's calendars containing English and Gujarati numbers, opportunities arose naturally to talk about the different ways in which the numbers 1 to 10 could be represented. Several children made their own calendars and their comments indicated that they were thinking about the languages involved. Ace copied English and Chinese numbers onto her calendar grid, with Colin helping with some of the English ones. Ace then showed her calendar to the whole class, reading out the Chinese numbers which she had learnt at home with her mother. Meera made calendars in both English and Gujarati, accompanied by Abbey, Michaela and Stefanie. On one particular day there was intense activity around calendars, with many children filling in the grids provided and pinning them up on the nursery walls.

Comparing the symbols used in different languages helped to emphasise the distinguishing characteristics of English letters and numbers. When Stefanie and Michaela, both monolingual, were working with a Gujarati alphabet book, Michaela found a letter similar to 'S' and commented 'S for your name, Stefanie'. As Stefanie traced the letter, I asked 'Is it the same?', to which she replied 'No, it's got something here' (a 'bar' across the S shape). I commented to her mother on Stefanie's interest in Gujarati and explained that the comparison between languages was helping to define the English alphabet for Stefanie.

### *Videos as a basis for literacy work*

Videos of different kinds were often children's favourite home literacy materials. The nursery had a weekly 'video time' for using the school's audiovisual facilities, and we made the multilingual materials part of this slot. The parents let us know which parts of the videos their children particularly liked and we used these short extracts to view with the class.

The videos held a number of literacy learning possibilities. Titles, credits and sub-titles appeared on the screen in different scripts. We could talk about the

**26**

*Figure 6: Song titles in Thai (from Billy's video, written by his mother) and in Tigrinya (from Marta's video, written by her father)*

*Figure 7: By Ace: 'The singers from Marta's video and Billy's video, their names, and some writing about the videos'*

writing used and how it linked to the spoken languages we heard, and ask children what they thought the writing might mean. Parents came into the classroom to make posters showing the title of the video or songs featured in it. Some of these posters were in English as well as the original language, so we could compare the two versions. After viewing the videos, children could 'write about the video', using the posters and the videocassette covers as a reference point (see Figs. 6 and 7). In some cases we invited another class in the school to come and watch the video with us; this involved making posters and invitations to advertise the event.

In these ways we explored the potential of a great variety of material which represented strong links with home for the bilingual children. This material was culturally very diverse and it was also diverse in type. We watched a Chinese video from Hong Kong in which a traditional story, 'Journey to the West', was re-configured as a cartoon for children living in the computer age. We saw Billy's karaoke video with songs in Thai, Marta's concert video with songs in Tigrinya, and Meera's Hindi blockbuster film which contained lively songs and dancing and about which her mother wrote in Gujarati. One of the monolingual children brought in her video copy of 'The Lion King' in English, and we were able to compare the English version of the theme song with its Spanish counterpart on Danny's audiotape.

In their responses, children seemed to be looking out for the markers of difference between written languages. They began commenting that they were

**27**

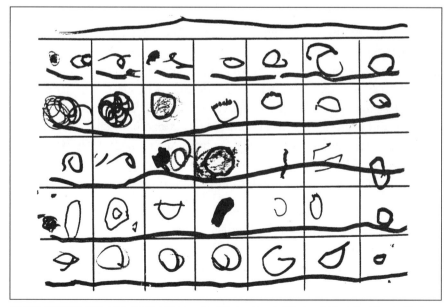

Figure 8: Michaela's grid, made after seeing Billy's video in Thai and Marta's video in Tigrinya. 'That's Billy's' (pointing to the top row) 'and that's Marta's' (pointing to the second row) 'and that says all Chinese' (pointing to one of the vertical columns)

writing in 'Chinese' or 'Spanish' for example, or specifically characterised their writing as 'English'. Although they wrote a whole variety of symbols which did not necessarily resemble any particular language, they had obviously realised that there were a whole variety of written languages. Sometimes they used several 'languages' in the same text. For example, Zubeadat filled a squared grid that could be used to make an alphabet or a calendar with many different symbols. One, which looked like 'I', she said was 'English', whilst the non-alphabetic character next to it was 'Spanish'. I asked if there was any Yoruba (her home language) and she pointed to a circle in the line of symbols below. Michaela, having recently seen the Thai and Tigrinya videos and being aware that Billy's and Marta's families spoke those languages, also filled up a grid, commenting 'It says, that's Billy's (pointing to the top row) and that's Marta's (pointing to another row) and that says all Chinese (indicating one of the vertical columns)' (see Fig.8).

After watching the Chinese video several times, some children showed that they could recognise the difference between Chinese and English script. Colin referred to a Chinese storybook and audiotape set as 'Ding Dong' (the title of the Chinese video). Adedamola read aloud from a Chinese magazine, saying 'ling ling ling', whereas when he came to an area of English script in the same magazine he responded by naming letters of the alphabet. Danielle noticed the Chinese characters written on a drinks can during a roleplay in the home corner and began offering 'Chinese drink' as part of her cafe menu. Ebony's mother reported her surprise when her daughter recognised some writing on the packaging of her toys as Chinese.

Children who had been learning to write their first languages at home already had a heightened awareness of these visual differences. When we watched the Chinese cartoon video for the first time, some children said the writing was 'English' but Ace – who had been working on Chinese with her mother – was clear that the script was Chinese. Mohammed, who was familiar with Arabic script from his lessons at home, could extend his visual awareness to new scripts. He was the only child apart from Ace to identify the writing on the screen as 'Chinese', and he was the only child to distinguish a piece of English writing that appeared in the cartoon as 'English'.

As well as gaining a sense of the visual appearance of different scripts and therefore of the characteristics of English writing, children became interested in specific symbols used in the videos. Colin and Ace wrote the Chinese characters for 'Ding Dong', the magic cat, on their invitations to another class to come and watch the cartoon. Michaela learned to differentiate between two song titles written in Thai and read them out correctly to Billy's mother. When Danny's mother was making the Spanish poster for 'The Lion King', Francis, Megan and Stefanie sat with her and each carefully wrote out

28

*Figure 9: Megan's poster inviting another class to come and see the video 'The Lion King' ('El Rey Leon' in Spanish). She added the clock face when I asked 'How will they know what time to come?'*

the title 'El Rey Leon' using her writing as a model (see Fig.9). Colin, who rarely attempted alphabet letters yet, wrote 'E l F R'. Stefanie, who found the task difficult too, not only finished 'El Rey Leon' in full but spent considerable time adding the song title 'Yo quisiera ser el rey' ('I just want to be King'). She also wrote some musical notes that Danny's mother had included in her poster. The challenge of different writing systems, combined with the fascination of the videos, inspired both monolingual and bilingual children to work closely on the details of written symbols.

### Topic work around multilingual texts

Another way we integrated multilingual work into the curriculum was through the class topic for each term. By the third term, Helen and I had built up a significant amount of information about the children's 'literacy worlds'. We were able to make this part of our planning around the topic of 'travel', which offered rich possibilities for bringing in different languages.

With the help of Sharon, the nursery nurse, we set up the home corner as a 'travel agency', with desks and chairs for the agents and customers, tickets and maps, plenty of writing materials, posters on the walls and a rack full of travel brochures for a good many countries. The whole class visited a local African-Caribbean-owned travel agency, saw the staff working at their computers and collected further tickets and brochures. Another possibility would have been to visit an agency run by Gujarati speakers, but it was a little further away.

The children surprised us with their understanding of the concept of long-distance travel. Several had already been on major journeys to see relatives in other countries, and the purpose of maps, tickets and brochures was quickly grasped throughout the nursery group. Many role-plays ensued in the home corner. Anthony packed his suitcase to leave for Jamaica, putting in leaflets and tickets along with a mobile phone. Jamel made a car out of bricks in the construction area and relived his holiday drive around Canada, while Zubeadat drew a map to use as the passenger. Ace, who knew that the London Underground map was for trains and 'which way they go', adapted the principle to a road map of Mexico City, tracing a route with her finger. Abbey offered various holidays to her clientele, ordering them to 'Get me one of those books (brochures) and tell me where you want to go', using the pictures to point out what they were going to see. She did not allow them to leave without the tickets she wrote out for them.

We encouraged the children, some bilingual and some monolingual, to make their own pages for a class 'travel brochure'. With the help of their parents, they could write about a place or country with which they had family connections. As well as cutting out illustrations from existing travel brochures, they could include family photos and pictures from the visits they had made. The pages were kept in a loose-leaf folder in the home corner so that they could be added to and used as part of play.

The brochure soon included Jamel's pages on Canada, Ace's pages on Hong Kong in Chinese and English, Meera's pages on India in Gujarati and English, and Billy's pages on Thailand in Thai and English. The pages made by Meera and Billy are discussed later in this book. Jamel's pages contained photos of a famous beauty spot in Canada, with a caption written by his mother, along with pictures of himself in a shopping centre and the flat where the family had stayed. He added his full name and the complete repertoire of numbers which he knew how to write, and the word 'Canada' which he wrote from an adult example.

Ace had a strong interest in her grandparents' country of origin, Hong Kong. When the nursery class visited the travel agency, we had been given a mobile advertising Hong Kong in Chinese writing. Ace immediately commented 'That's where I come from, and my mum, and her mum'. She helped to hang up the mobile in the home corner 'travel agency'. She wanted to look at a brochure for Hong Kong, saying 'I want that one, that's where I come from'. To make Ace's own travel brochure page, her mother wrote 'Hong Kong' in Chinese and Ace cut out photos from the professional brochure, choosing pictures of a young woman's face and an elegant skyscraper. She also wrote 'Hong Kong' in English from her mother's example; the letter 'K' caused her some difficulty, and she had to trace several example 'K's' of mine in order to accomplish it.

**31**

The travel brochure pages gave children the opportunity to display their knowledge about other countries and extend their writing repertoire. The writing of 'Hong Kong', for example, interested Ace and she pointed out that the two 'G's' in the words were the same letter. A month later, Ace showed that she had noted the form of these words – when Michaela included a 'p' in her writing of 'Hong Kong', Ace insisted 'That doesn't say Hong Kong – Hong Kong hasn't got a P'.

Another activity we were able to integrate into the 'travel' topic was the writing of airletters by parents. This was an important aspect of several children's home literacy experience, and Helen and I were keen to make connections with the activity in order to help children's learning. We provided blue airletter forms and asked parents if they could sit in the nursery and show how they would write a letter to relatives in other countries. Our plan was to ask for pictures and information from each family's country of origin, which could be used as part of the travel brochure.

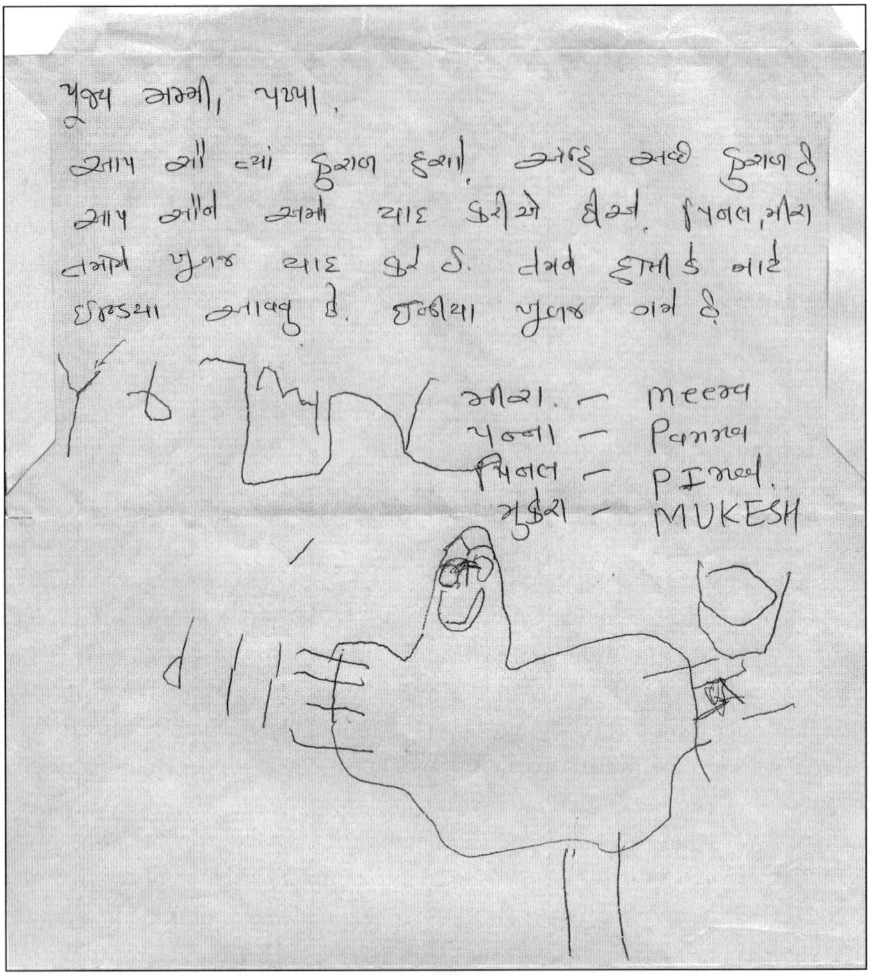

Figure 10: Airletter in Gujarati, written by Meera's mother in the nursery
(with additions by Meera, later that morning)

Several parents did as we asked, with their children sitting beside them and often writing airletters too. The distinctive airletter forms and airmail paper aroused considerable interest among the children. Meera recognised the blue envelopes familiar from home and observed that 'My mum's got those'. The materials remained available for children to use in the writing area after the parents left.

Once again, the experience of seeing their parents write in the classroom led children to write along with them and afterwards. Meera began using her own airletter form alongside her mother (see Figs.10 and 11). She covered the whole page with print, like an authentic letter writer. Recognising that Gujarati script was appropriate for a letter to India, she began with some Gujarati symbols she knew – the first two letters of the name of her video, which appeared on a poster made by her mother and displayed on the nursery

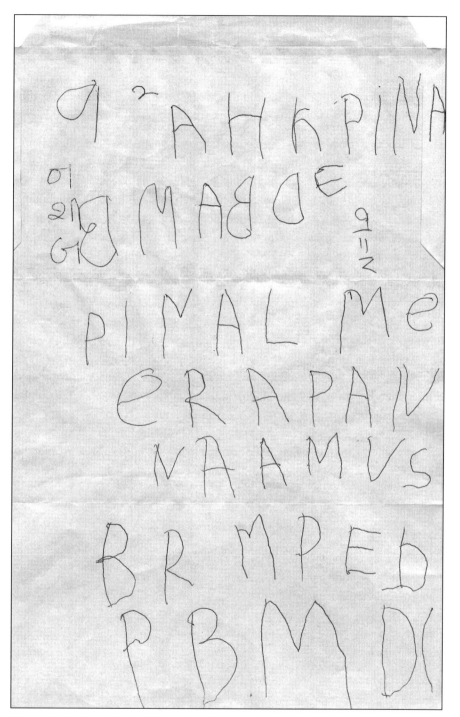

*Figure 11: Airletter written by Meera, alongside her mother in the nursery. Meera's comments:*
*– top left-hand symbol: 'That says India ... that's my film'*
*– English alphabet letters: 'That says India, that's my shop' and names of her family*

wall. Later Meera commented about these symbols 'That says India – that's my film'. She continued with seven lines of English alphabet letters, including the family names from her mother's airletter. About the English letters she said 'That says India, that's my shop'. She seemed to understand that a letter to India could give news about the small supermarket run by her family in London, and that the family's names would also be included.

The airletter gave Meera the chance to extend her writing in both English and Gujarati. She could already write her own name and her sister's in English unaided, but in the letter she also wrote her parents' names and then read all the family names back to me. Later, she added to her mother's airletter, using her mother's writing as a model to produce several Gujarati symbols new to her. Over the next month, Meera wrote several more airletters, including family names in English, and experimented with Gujarati writing.

Marta responded in some similar ways, although she was nine months younger than Meera and not yet writing as much. Her father was not aware that Marta had noticed him writing letters to Eritrea at home, yet when he sat down to write an airletter in Tigrinya in the nursery, Marta wanted to join in. She went round proudly showing her letter to the nursery staff. That afternoon she showed her letter and her father's to the whole nursery group, and immediately sat down to write again, with both texts to hand. Marta's original **34** letter mostly consisted of short vertical lines with a few other marks (like Meera, she may have wanted to cover the page quickly), whereas her second text contained a variety of more developed symbols. Her father told me two weeks later that she had been writing more at home.

*Parents and children at a multilingual newspaper workshop in school*

## Multilingual literacy work in other early years classes

Bilingual and monolingual children all benefited from the flexible learning environment of the nursery and the ideas about writing in different languages. Teachers may wonder to what extent they can pursue this kind of multilingual work in the more structured curriculum for 5 year olds upwards. Many of the activities described above could be planned into National Literacy Strategy sessions: helping children discuss how written language works (from alphabet and number systems to words and sentences), and how different types of text are structured (letters, brochures, calendars, posters, invitations). As the examples here show, different languages and different kinds of literacy materials can become a resource for lively debate.

Another possibility is to organise specific sessions around particular literacy materials. As children in the nursery class moved on to Reception, I continued to work with them. Their new teacher, Sarah, had long experience of making bilingualism a part of classroom learning. As part of a weekly Language Workshop, we ran sessions in which bilingual families brought in newspapers from home in languages ranging from Portuguese and Turkish to Gujarati and Urdu. Children were encouraged to make their own newspapers on large folded sheets of paper, cutting out items from the original newspapers and surrounding them with their own writing. Parents and other family members were there to help. These workshops were highly productive over an entire school year, with monolingual children again showing great interest in using home literacy materials and writing in different languages. The design and layout of newspapers from different countries, and the subject matter, held considerable potential for comparison with the structure of English newspapers.

**35**

Such sessions could also be organised as part of family literacy work, a growing area of education throughout the country that often operates in school premises. Family literacy is based on the concept of encouraging parents and children to develop their skills and confidence around literacy together, thus involving parents more closely in their children's education. Bilingual work of this kind has proved to have great benefits (see for instance Green, 1999).

## Issues which arise in a multilingual classroom

The multilingual work described is an unusual experience for most parents and children. It is taking place within a society which generally tends to ignore or discourage bilingualism. There are therefore some important issues to bear in mind when using home texts and inviting parents to write in the classroom. One is the need to 'protect' multilingual texts in a monolingual school system. Another is ensuring that parents receive appropriate support as writers in school. And finally, careful negotiation is needed with parents when establishing multilingual literacy work. These issues are now discussed in more detail.

## Making the classroom a 'safe place' for home texts

Bilingual texts are not part of the mainstream in a society which accepts monolingualism as the norm and are therefore potentially vulnerable within school. Bilingual children very soon become aware that society accords greater power to the English language and those who write it. Among the nursery children, Meera and Ace showed a particular awareness of this situation. Meera asked numerous times for her video to be shown again, but also expressed concern that children had laughed 'too much' at the slapstick sequence. And when some children laughed at the writing on Billy's video, Ace said emphatically 'It's not funny'.

However, Meera and Ace were able to work productively with Gujarati and Chinese texts in the nursery, because their teacher's explicit commitment to multilingual writing accorded high status to home literacy materials. Meera followed her own agenda to investigate Gujarati script throughout the school year, as related later. And in a multilingual literacy environment, Ace was able to explore her sense of Chinese as well as English identity at school. During one of the multilingual video sessions, she commented 'I'm a Chinese girl, aren't I, and I'm an English girl too'. Looking at the airletter written in Gujarati by Meera's mother on another occasion, she announced 'My mum's Chinese – I'm a little Chinese girl'. From the age of 3 or even earlier, particularly because of sessions of writing Chinese at home, Ace was conscious that her mother wanted her to feel connected with her Chinese background. Her comments show that she understood her mother's concerns and had decided to claim a Chinese identity for herself. The nursery classroom was a safe place in which to do so.

## A sensitive approach to parents as writers

Particular sensitivity is required of teachers about the parents' own confidence in their ability to write in home languages. For example, one of the nursery parents who had been brought up in Britain and attended community language classes as a child wanted her daughter to have the chance to become literate in her family's language, but felt unsure about writing in the nursery. We introduced her to another adult who shared her language and could work alongside her in the classroom. We also encouraged her to base her writing on literacy materials such as newspapers which were right there in the nursery. So we were able to offer her positive support.

Another parent, who was not literate in Urdu, wanted to learn – and the newspaper workshop provided the ideal opportunity to start. The atmosphere was relaxed and friendly. Sitting alongside children and adults who were experimenting with many different languages, she could try out Urdu writing with no risk of criticism. In fact, her 5 year old daughter confidently took charge and showed her mother 'you do it like this'. Mother and daughter wrote together.

### *Negotiating with parents around multilingual work*

Parents themselves may feel unsure at first about their children learning to write in more than one language. Often they have absorbed messages from the society around them that bilingualism is 'problematic', and that it is 'too hard' for young children to become literate in another language as well as English. It is not very long since schools were sending letters home asking parents to speak only English with their children, a policy which is now known to be totally misguided. In the nursery, we sometimes needed to explain to parents that the research overwhelmingly shows bilingualism and biliteracy to be advantageous and they were surprised to hear this. As we demonstrated our belief in the research evidence through our commitment to bilingual learning in the classroom, parents who were initially unsure became more confident about providing home literacy materials and participating in activities.

At the same time, we needed to be aware of parents' own literacy agendas for their children and respect them when we made suggestions for classroom work. We also took care when bringing literacy materials in different languages into the nursery ourselves, showing them to the parents first for their opinion and comments. It was important that the parents should see the multilingual work as a joint enterprise to which they could contribute, rather than as imposed by the school.

### Issues which arise in a largely monolingual classroom

Many bilingual children are learning in settings which are rather different from the multilingual classrooms described here. They may be among only a handful of children who speak more than one language in an otherwise monolingual, monocultural class. They may indeed be the only bilingual child in the class. Can such classrooms become multilingual literacy environments?

The work discussed in this chapter clearly demonstrates that monolingual children show considerable interest in writing in different languages. Young children are trying to find out how writing operates in general and asking themselves 'what do marks on paper stand for?' Different scripts are a source of fascination and provide new ways of answering the question. If bilingual children and their parents are invited to contribute their knowledge as part of the learning enterprise, this will at the same time raise the status of home languages in the classroom. Meanwhile, teachers can keep monolingual parents informed about the purpose of the multilingual literacy work and how it can add extra motivation for their children's learning.

The monolingual parents in our classrooms were impressed by their children's participation in writing languages such as Chinese and Gujarati at such an early age. We explained that these activities were helping their children to understand more about how writing works. The parents' positive response helped to build a supportive atmosphere for bilingual learning in the school.

## New literacy practices in the classroom

Having taken certain steps to ensure that home texts were 'protected' in school and that families felt comfortable about participating, we were engaged, together with the bilingual parents and children, on a voyage which would inevitably proceed in new directions. Literacy activities in the classroom were bound to differ in some ways from reading and writing activities at home. We were not trying to replicate home literacy practices, however, but rather to make fruitful connections with children's home experience. And it proved possible to do so.

Parents were able to adapt to classroom situations. Writing an airletter at a table surrounded by excited nursery children, for example, was a very different experience from sitting quietly at home. At first, parents offered to write their airletters at home, but when we asked if they could also write a letter in the classroom 'for the children to use in the nursery', they were happy to do so. Our request made sense to them because they knew that the children were using bilingual texts for learning at school and also that the airletters were being written for a purpose, as part of the nursery's topic work.

Just as writing in the school environment presented a different experience for the parents, it also offered new possibilities for the children as writers. In the case of the airletters, for example, they had access to their own supply of airletter forms, and could retain their parent's airletter, write on it, and use it as a stimulus for further writing. At home the letter would have disappeared into the postbox and no longer be available for reference. Children became accustomed to experimenting with written language in the nursery, using home texts as a resource.

Thus the family airletter had been given purpose and status in the nursery and turned into 'home-school literacy material'. New material of this kind became the basis for children to generate further pieces of writing and reflect on how literacy worked. The process which we used to build connections between home and school literacy in the nursery is represented below (see Fig.12). From our experience, the new directions taken were successful. Multilingual work in the classroom offered support to parents who were

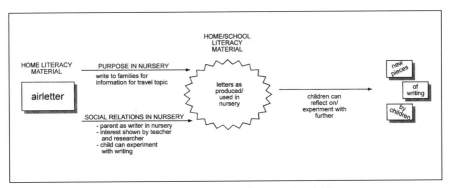

*Figure 12: Building links between home and social literacy*

already teaching their children to write in different languages, gave educational credibility to biliteracy for parents who were unsure about its value, and provided opportunities for children to become emergent bilingual writers. The following chapters describe in detail how particular children took up those opportunities to enhance their literacy learning.

## Ideas for creating a multilingual literacy environment at school

- You could suggest a staff discussion of your school's language policy to check how it relates to bilingual learning. For example, does it clearly state that bilingualism is educationally advantageous? Does it say that bilingual learning is welcomed and encouraged at school? Maggie Gravelle's book *Supporting Bilingual Learners in Schools* (1996) outlines the issues to cover in a language policy.

- The school could hold a meeting open to parents and the community to talk about 'the advantages of learning in more than one language'. If the meeting is publicised by word of mouth, and parents know that interpreters will be present, you may draw a surprisingly large audience. It's important that the head teacher is present to confirm the school's support for bilingualism.

- When inviting parents to bring materials in different languages from home into school, you can talk about the advantages of biliteracy and explain that children will be using the materials to help their learning. Some parents will already have a strong desire for their children to be biliterate, but others will need your reassurance.

- When families bring home literacy materials into school, these need to be given a prominent place in the classroom. Book racks in the reading area can contain a variety of texts as well as storybooks, written in a range of relevant languages – including English. Display boards in the writing area and home corner can include writing by parents and children in their home languages.

- When parents and other family members come in to write in the nursery, make sure there is plenty of support (home language texts to refer to, parents who write the same language alongside them). Even when parents do not actually write in a particular language, they may read it (e.g. Arabic used as a religious language) or be able to tell you what the text is about. Every bilingual household will have a relationship to literacy.

- Encourage children to experiment with multilingual writing as part of home corner play and in the writing area. The National Literacy Strategy requires children to become confident writers of text of many types, and specifically mentions that pupils should be able to explore writing through play situations (1998, p. 19). Ask children to show their experimental writing to the whole class so that you can talk about it together.

- Comparisons between different languages can be a regular feature of the Literacy Hour. The National Literacy Strategy requires children to investigate language at the word, sentence and text level. Home texts can be used to show examples, and parents and children can help you. Their contributions will hold the interest of other children and help to increase language awareness. Here are some ideas:

  *Word level* – children can compare different alphabets and writing systems. How do symbols relate to sounds in each language? Which are the same as in the English system and which are different? Norah McWilliam's book *What's in a Word?* (1998) offers plenty of ideas for helping children to look at word meaning in different languages, such as talking about the homonyms they know in their first languages as well as English.

  *Sentence level* – even very young children are likely to be aware that word order differs between English and other languages they know. For example, in many languages the adjective comes after the noun: 'cat black' not 'black cat'. Punctuation symbols can also be compared in different languages – in Spanish, an 'upside-down' question mark appears at the beginning of each question.

  *Text level* – texts such as letters and newspapers may be organised and laid out in different ways in different languages/countries. What characterises each one?

- Keep up a dialogue with parents about how home literacy materials have been used in the classroom. Invite them in to see what their children have been working on that day, and ask about any writing children may have done at home. Include the monolingual parents and explain how their children's interest in different languages can help their literacy learning.

40

# CHAPTER THREE

# Billy and Recep:
# Finding a Role as Writers

Teachers quite commonly find children 'reluctant to write'. When faced with pen and paper, they tend to find other diversions, stare at the page, and finally produce one or two marks at the teacher's insistence. They seem to have no desire to write.

But this could be just because some classroom tasks have no obvious connection with the purposeful writing children observe in their homes and communities. Perhaps the topics which are dearest to their heart and which they would like to write about, are not part of the school agenda. The same children can be transformed when they have the chance to write on their own terms – to find a role as writers.

I particularly remember Carlie, a 5 year old in a Reception class I visited. It was Monday morning and everyone was sitting at tables with their writing books in front of them. They had been asked, as they were at the beginning of every week, to write their 'news' from the weekend. Carlie did not seem to feel that she had much to tell that was newsworthy in classroom terms. When I asked what she had done at the weekend she said 'I went to the shop'. It so happened that I knew Carlie's older brother and her mother, so I mentioned this to her and asked if she could draw her dad for me, since he was the only member of the family I had not met. She did the drawing with enthusiasm and then began to write. Once she began, she wrote long strings of letters, saying 'This is how I write Carlie, and that's how my teacher writes it'. She wrote her first name and her family name, and 'Dad'.

Later, when I was walking through the school hall, I met Carlie's mother, who worked in the school as a primary helper. When I mentioned Carlie's interest in writing her name, she smiled and remarked that Carlie liked to do it differently. She also told me that Carlie wrote a great deal at home – she had a little table to sit at and pens of her own to use. She had written a list of her friends' names that morning, which Carlie's mother pulled out of her pocket to show to me.

I was struck by discovering that Carlie was such a productive writer at home. Her mother thought that her daughter's teacher probably did not know this. Intriguingly, Carlie's home writing was right there in the school, in her mother's pocket, yet her teacher was unlikely to know that either. Although parent and teacher saw each other each day, home literacy was not a topic of conversation. Ultimately, the opportunity to write about her family in the classroom tapped into Carlie's interests and showed that her status as a 'reluctant writer' did not have to become permanent.

## Motivations for writing in the nursery

Writing in the home corner was very popular in the nursery where my research was based. We often had to replenish the stocks of paper and envelopes; sometimes they were used up by lunchtime. Writing events ranged from those where children worked individually or in pairs, to large-scale dramatic games in which many of them participated, such as the day when I noticed Ace sitting in bed in the home corner writing on computer paper, while the others brought her cards and put their writing and pictures up on the wall.

According to the parents, their children displayed similar enthusiasm for literacy activities at home. All the parents I interviewed described their children as intensely interested in observing writing by siblings and adults and in producing writing of their own. Ebony would try to take the pen and paper out of her mother's hands when any writing was going on; Stefanie would write whenever 'anyone has a pen'; Colin wrote as part of play with his sister; Vanessa was in tears when she lost the pencil case her brother had bought her.

In the nursery it was often the boys who seemed less enthusiastic when asked to do writing tasks. They were generally more interested in noisy, active play and found it harder to sit down and concentrate. However, opportunities to write as part of home corner play could be attractive. Colin set up a 'bank' in the home corner, where he kept papers in a small chest of drawers. His customers had to exchange a piece of written text for money: as Colin explained to Ian 'You write a letter, you give to me in the bank and you get five pounds back'. The 'bank' was also the venue for Colin to instruct me to fill in forms or put notes in envelopes so I could receive toys and dressing-up clothes in return. One morning I observed Colin going to and from the home corner carrying a folder. He told me 'I'm going to my lunch – back in three minutes'. Running his bank gave Colin a feeling of importance and a chance to explore some of the many literacy activities he had observed in the wider world.

Similarly, Curtis used the home corner 'travel agency' as the office for a mini-cab service: 'sit down and I'll get you a cab'. He also wrote out messages such as 'go in the cab to the hospital'. Hamish and Francis spent a long time in a 'cafe' role-play during which they produced menus, described by Francis as 'a diagram, what you want to eat – of all the... spaghetti bolognese... cheese... and breakfast'. Adedamola and Ian were part of a group perusing catalogues for toys and filling in order forms in the home corner. All these activities enabled children to take a leading part in using literacy for purposes which connected strongly with their home experience.

For bilingual children, home life would include many of the everyday activities just described. However, these might involve languages additional to English, and experiences with which home corner role-plays might not immediately connect. This was why it was important to have abundant multilingual home literacy materials in the classroom and to involve parents as writers. Billy and Recep were two of the children – both of them boys – who blossomed when a direct connection was made with their home languages and literacy practices. This was apparent from Billy's response to his mother's airletter writing in the nursery, and Recep's response to the newspaper workshops in his Year 1 class.

## Billy and the airletters

Billy's 'literacy world' was described in the first chapter of this book. You may remember that his mother was trying to teach him the alphabet in both Thai and English. She commented to us that she was worried because Billy was not writing much at home. The teacher and I had noticed that Billy did not write often in the nursery either, beyond one or two letters of his name. In conversation with Billy's mother, it emerged that the only time Billy showed enthusiasm for writing at home was when he sat next to her while she wrote letters to the family in Thailand.

When we planned the letter-writing activities in the nursery, linked with children's home experience, Billy's mother was one of the parents who participated. When offered his own airletter form to use, Billy was keen to join in. His mother wrote several lines of Thai script on her airletter, as if writing to Billy's grandmother, while Billy filled his airletter with lines and symbols in different colours. As mother and son wrote, they conversed in Thai and English. Their talk linked their writing to its purpose – communicating with family who lived far away.

I asked Billy if he wanted to sign his mother's letter but he said he wanted his mother to write his name, so she wrote 'Billy' on a separate piece of paper in English. Billy was not yet confident about writing his name in full, so his mother provided a model for him to use in English as well as a model of writing an airletter in Thai. Both models were to prove fruitful for Billy's literacy development.

### 'I write like my mum'

Later the same morning, after his mother had gone home, Billy came to the writing table and spent about fifteen minutes there – unusually long for him. Even when the rest of the class gathered on the carpet for 'group time', Billy wanted to remain at the table. He wrote on strips of computer paper with punched holes along the edge, that had been put out for the children to experiment with and which he particularly seemed to like. His mother had written his name on the same kind of paper earlier. As he began, Billy said 'I write like my mum'. In one of his texts, he included some complex symbols and commented 'Mu-ang Thai' ('Thailand'). These did not resemble English alphabet letters – they looked more like his mother's Thai symbols (see Fig.13). The recognition of Billy's mother as a bilingual writer in the nursery seemed to have inspired him to want to be a writer in Thai too.

On the same afternoon, Billy again used his mother's writing as a resource, this time in English. As before, he came voluntarily to the writing table, where he began drawing round some plastic alphabet letters kept there. With Michaela's help, he identified 'B' for 'Billy'. We looked at his mother's writing of his name, and I helped him to find each letter among the basketful of plastic alphabet letters. He drew carefully round all of them. Afterwards he chose a place on the home corner walls to put up the texts written by him and his mother that day. This was a public display of Billy's prowess as an emergent bilingual writer.

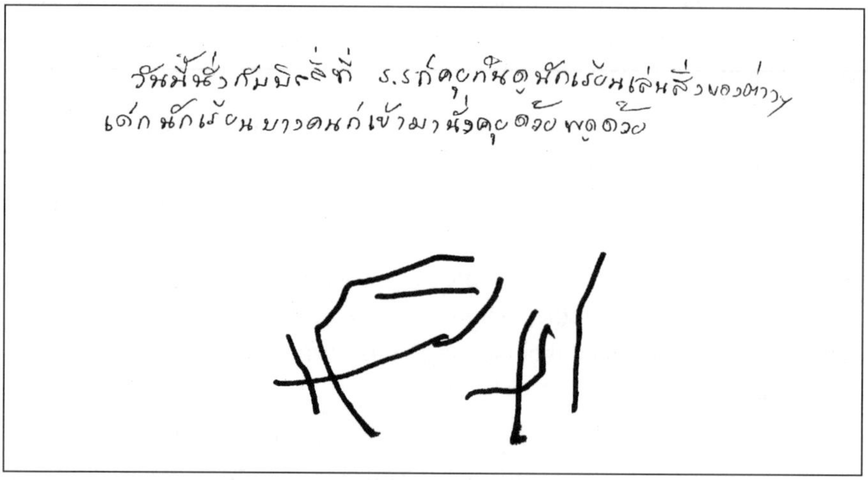

*Figure 13: (above) extract from airletter in Thai, written by Billy's mother in the nursery (below) symbols written by Billy later that morning – he said 'I write like my mum' 'Mu-ang Thai'*

## Links between home and school writing

The following week, Billy's mother told us with pleasure that he was writing far more at home. Sharing her excitement, we encouraged her to bring anything he wrote at home into school to show us. A few days later she appeared with a plastic carrier bag containing twenty-one pieces of writing! The fact that she volunteered information about what Billy was doing at home and collected his writing to bring to school showed that she perceived home and school as connected sites for literacy learning.

Billy's writing was impressive in amount and scale. The twenty-one texts had all been written in the space of a few days. He was writing on any materials that came to hand – McDonald's placemats, official letters, computer paper brought from school to home. The symbols he used were extremely varied: English alphabet letters and numbers, repeated circles, some complex symbols which looked like Thai, and drawings of people. It was as if the floodgates had opened – Billy was experimenting with many different kinds of representation. Indeed, his mother said that both his writing and drawing were new to her; she had not seen him drawing people before.

Some of Billy's writing was connected with his family, an important source of inspiration. When writing symbols on computer paper he had said to his mother 'Mummy, Daddy'. His drawings on a McDonalds leaflet were identified as 'Mum, Dad, me'. As well as covering large sheets of paper with letters from his own name, he included the first letters of his parents' and sister's names. We were surprised to see that he could now write the first three letters of 'Billy' confidently by himself. For other family names, he used his mother's writing as a reference.

As his mother and I sat looking at Billy's texts in the classroom, Billy came up to show us his work and talk about it with pride. This of course gave him further status as a writer with the nursery staff. And the flow of writing continued. Three days later, his mother brought in another bag containing twenty-seven more pieces of work. She commented 'He's writing in the morning, at breakfast!' Billy had been transformed from a reluctant writer into one who was hard to stop.

In these new pieces, Billy had continued to develop his writing of different symbols, both alone and with the help of other people. He was now producing initials from family names all by himself, and he also participated in writing alphabet letters with an adult friend. He had written numbers based on his mother's model and done his own on another sheet of paper. This time, a line of Thai letters was evident in a notebook – his mother had helped him to copy them. When he showed them to me, Billy told me 'Mu-ang Thai' ('Thailand'). Was he now happier to benefit from his mother's instruction at

45

home, because Thai writing had been publicly admired and displayed in the nursery?

Again, Billy came over to comment on his work when his mother and I were looking at it together. He talked at length about each page and wrote the letter 'B' on several of them, as if adding his signature. He had clearly become a more confident writer in the nursery. He would spend time looking through baskets of wooden and plastic letters in order to draw a selection, and I saw him call Meera over to see his writing of his name.

As well as writing family names at home, Billy had asked his mother how to write 'Helen' and 'Sharon', the names of his teacher and the nursery nurse. In a little writing book taken home from school, he had incorporated 'H' and 'S' alongside letters from 'Billy'. His writing represented a link between himself and the nursery staff.

Another link between home and school was established when Billy's mother showed us a birthday card sent to Billy from Thailand. In the card was a message from his aunt in Thai, and Billy had added his own writing underneath. Billy's mother brought the birthday card to school in his book folder, which was designed to take home reading books from the classroom. She had thought it appropriate to use the folder also to bring texts from home to school. Thus the one-way school-home pathway was transformed into a route for two-way traffic.

Throughout this time, there was an interplay between home and school in Billy's writing development, as shown below (Fig.14). A home literacy activity, writing airletters, had been a springboard for joint writing by Billy and his mother in the nursery. This led to Billy doing more writing at home and this was talked about and commented on at school. A further burst of work at home was also shown to the nursery staff. And when Billy's birthday card was brought to the classroom this confirmed the home-school connection.

## Billy's travel brochure pages

The pages Billy and his mother made together to contribute to the nursery's 'travel brochure' provided yet another reference to home and stimulus for writing. On the first page was 'Thailand', written in Thai and English by Billy's mother, some symbols written in the same colour pen by Billy, and a map of the country which he cut out carefully from a real travel brochure. For the second page, Billy chose further pictures to cut out and stick in, showing a temple, a statue of a dragon, a floating market, and Thai dancers. We then found out the cost of an air ticket to Thailand – £479 – and Billy's mother helped him to write it in, using her own writing as a model.

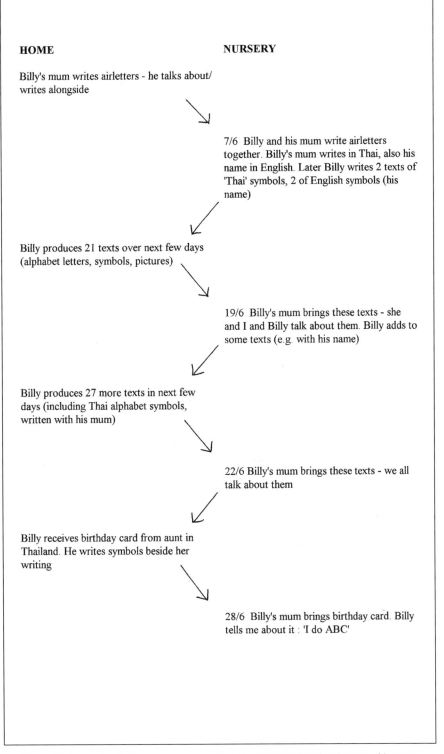

HOME

NURSERY

Billy's mum writes airletters - he talks about/
writes alongside

7/6  Billy and his mum write airletters
together. Billy's mum writes in Thai, also his
name in English. Later Billy writes 2 texts of
'Thai' symbols, 2 of English symbols (his
name)

Billy produces 21 texts over next few days
(alphabet letters, symbols, pictures)

19/6  Billy's mum brings these texts - she
and I and Billy talk about them. Billy adds to
some texts (e.g. with his name)

Billy produces 27 more texts in next few
days (including Thai alphabet symbols,
written with his mum)

22/6 Billy's mum brings these texts - we all
talk about them

Billy receives birthday card from aunt in
Thailand. He writes symbols beside her
writing

28/6  Billy's mum brings birthday card. Billy
tells me about it : 'I do ABC'

**47**

*Figure 14: Interaction between home and school in Billy's writing development (dates are given for events at school)*

Both Billy's parents came into the nursery that morning and sat with him, encouraging him to help with the brochure. This visit gave them the opportunity to discuss Billy's language and literacy development with the teacher. A couple of days later, his father brought in several family photographs to add to the brochure. They showed Billy as a baby in Thailand, playing with his aunt and sitting on his grandmother's knee surrounded by his cousins. Another photo was of a prayer meeting with a group of monks dressed in saffron-coloured robes, about which Billy commented 'Mu-ang Thai'. Billy stuck these pictures into the travel brochure folder to make new pages.

The brochure was a tangible realisation of Billy's family life, combining photographs of his relatives and events in Thailand with writing by his mother and himself. It exemplified Billy's knowledge about the world and about literacy: when showing his pages to the whole class, Billy identified his own writing ('I did that') and explained that his mother's writing of 'Thailand' referred to the map. In the flexible literacy environment of the nursery, Billy could keep up a dialogue over his brochure pages through talking and writing. He returned to the folder in the home corner several times. Once he took out his three pages to look at and talk about, then put them back later. Another time he commented 'Billy's' and 'Mu-ang Thai' (Thailand), and added letters from his name in English to one of the pages. Two days later he pointed out his writing of his name to his mother, as they looked at the brochure together and talked about going to Thailand.

Like the airletters, the brochure pages seemed to provide a continual home presence for Billy in the nursery, giving him an opportunity to represent the areas of his life which were specifically connected with Thai language and literacy. From this position of strength, he also gained the confidence and desire to write about himself in English.

## Recep's newspapers

Recep was another child who found a role for himself as a writer when given the chance to refer to his home experience in the classroom. He had not been part of the original research project in the nursery, joining the school in the Reception class at the age of 4. His teacher, Sarah, was constantly looking for opportunities for children to engage in bilingual learning and it was at this point that she and I began to organise weekly Language Workshops. As described in the last chapter, parents and children brought in newspapers in different languages and made their own newspapers together in the classroom.

Sarah had noticed that although Recep took part enthusiastically in most classroom activities, he was not always keen to write. When I asked him 'Does anyone in your family write in Turkish?' he immediately replied 'My grandmother'. I asked if he could show me how she wrote and he promptly began to cover a large poster-sized sheet of paper with symbols. Recep continued writing for the rest of that session and did not want to go out at playtime because, he said, 'I haven't finished'. The connection with Turkish seemed to have unlocked a door into Recep's literacy world, which was potentially vast.

Recep's enthusiasm continued when he brought Turkish newspapers from home into school and made his own newspapers with the help of his mother and his aunt. As Recep chose images and text to cut out from the newspapers, it became obvious that he was familiar with the contents. He pointed out his favourite singer, wrote her name under her picture with adult help and sang us lines from her songs. He cut out a photo of star actors from a soap opera he watched on Turkish satellite TV and carefully copied several lines from the accompanying text (see Fig.15). His interest in Turkish football was considerable; a dramatic picture of two players challenging each other for the ball provided another source for his writing.

From his TV experience and education within his family, Recep also had a greater knowledge of news events and history than might have been expected from a 5 year old. In the central position on the front cover of his newspaper he placed a striking picture of the French prime minister, Jacques Chirac, bending over to kiss the hand of Tansu Çiller, who was then prime minister of Turkey. Recep included the caption below the picture which highlighted Çiller's name and appeared to know that she was an important person in

**49**

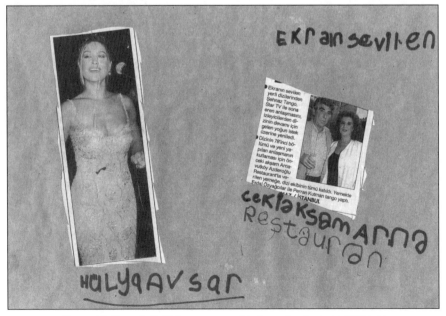

*Figure 15: Recep's Turkish newspaper: his favourite singer and TV soap*

Turkey. He also recognised the picture of Atatürk, the founder of Turkey, which appeared alongside the banner headline of one of the newspapers, and asked his aunt to help him write the name 'Atatürk' above the headline. It emerged that Recep had a book about Atatürk at home. Again, tapping into this knowledge gave Recep reason to write in school.

The representation of news, cultural and sporting events in Recep's newspaper was completely intermingled with writing about his family. He wrote his mother's name, 'Halide', next to 'Atatürk' and put his sister's name, 'Gülten', and a drawing of her alongside the picture of Tansu Çiller on the front page (see Fig.16). For Recep these were all part and parcel of his home life. He was eager to put every aspect of his family and community experience into writing.

This intermingling of different aspects continued when Recep brought his family photo album to the multilingual newspaper sessions. He showed the pictures to other children and parents and talked about his visits to Cyprus. He drew an accurate outline of the island of Cyprus based on a postcard map in his album and, below it, a picture of his grandfather in a coffin with flowers. He explained to me that his grandfather had died and gone up into the sky. His father later told me that the funeral in Cyprus had made a strong impression on Recep, even though he had been only 3 years old at the time. The drawing of the map and the picture held a linked importance for Recep – both were significant reasons for making his own text.

**50**

*Figure 16: Recep's Turkish newspaper: the Prime Minister and Recep's sister Gülten*

Turkish was not the only language which Recep put in his newspaper. Like many of the bilingual and monolingual children who joined in with the newspaper sessions, he was fascinated by languages not his own. He included excerpts from Chinese newspapers and did some detailed writing of Chinese using these characters as models. This demonstrated his interest in different writing systems and his fascination with how to write individual symbols. Such attention to detail is a crucial part of early literacy learning for all children.

Recep was paying attention to all levels of text as specified in the National Literacy Strategy – from word level (individual symbols as just described, and the names of his family and famous Turkish people) to sentence level (the lines he wrote based on the newspaper text) and text level (the overall design of his newspaper pages and the suitably varied contents of news, entertainment and sport). His ability to do all this only became evident because his teacher and I had taken such interest in his home literacy experience and given it a significant place within the classroom.

For both Billy and Recep, the presence of home texts and the support of their parents played a key part in encouraging them to write at school. The multilingual literacy environment gave them the chance to write from what they knew, about what they knew – with teachers who respected their knowledge and affirmed them in their role as emergent bilingual writers.

**51**

## Ideas for encouraging children as writers

- As part of whole-class discussions (ranging from topic work and language work to 'what did you do at the weekend?'), you can invite bilingual children to talk about anything they have been reading or writing at home in any language. You can make it clear that you are interested in all sorts of activities: for example, have they watched cable or satellite TV in a home language? have they got any tapes or videos? have they seen parents or grandparents reading a newspaper?

- Children may be shy about mentioning their home language literacy activities until a multilingual literacy environment begins to be established in the classroom. Once they see their teacher working with texts in a number of languages, they will have evidence that bilingualism is part of school learning and they will feel comfortable about telling you what they know.

- Monolingual children will probably want to have something 'special' to talk about too. They are likely to add their own language and literacy experiences to the discussion (for example, when we worked with the 'Lion King' audio-book in Spanish in the nursery, another child brought in her 'Lion King' video in English and we used both). This is a valuable way of finding out more about the home knowledge of all the children in the class.

- You could ask children whether anyone in their family writes in any language besides English. An open-ended question such as 'Can you show me how your grandmother writes?' or 'Would you like to do some writing in Chinese/Turkish....?' can stimulate children to engage in emergent writing. The presence in class of materials in their home language is a great support, particularly if the children themselves have brought in their favourite items (such as Recep's photo album).

- The 'reading folder' which children take to and from school can be used for a two-way exchange of literacy items. As well as taking storybooks home from the classroom, children can be encouraged to bring in anything they have been reading at home. This will help teachers to find out about the immense variety of literacy activities the children enjoy. In our experience in the nursery, items which might appear in the folder can range from leaflets and cereal packets to Chinese storybooks, Indian film magazines and Billy's birthday card from Thailand. The reading folder gives status to the materials carried in it and shows that home literacy is considered important in the classroom.

**52**

- A similar two-way exchange can be established with writing done at home and at school. If the teacher shows examples of children's emergent writing done in the classroom, parents will realise that emergent writing done at home is of interest to the school and be encouraged to bring in examples, either in a carrier bag as Billy's mother did, or in the reading folder or similar 'writing folder'. Children will soon choose items they want to bring into school.

- Time spent on family literacy workshops, like the newspaper sessions described in this chapter, will reap ample rewards. The workshops forge closer relationships between teachers and parents and provide informal opportunities to discuss children's learning. They are an excellent way of enabling parents and children to write together in school.

# CHAPTER FOUR

# Meera's Story:
# Investigating Written Languages

It was a remark by the school's Language Co-ordinator that set me on the path of this research with children in the nursery. 'It would be interesting' she said, 'to find out what children think about different scripts at the age when they are just beginning to learn what writing is'. This struck me as an important and fascinating question. When I went on to plan the research, some people suggested that 4 year olds would be too young to have noticed differences between scripts or to be thinking about how written language operates.

I was optimistic. Previous experiences with young bilingual children in primary school had revealed to me the understandings shown by 5 year olds about the existence of different spoken languages. When I began speaking in Spanish to one class, explaining that the word for book was 'libro', the monolingual children were astonished to find that an object could have more than one name. I was besieged by children pointing to windows, doors and tables and asking 'What's that called in Spanish?' The bilingual children approached the situation more calmly; they already knew about this linguistic difference and had probably been quietly cogitating on it for some time. When asked, they offered translations in their own languages. So it seemed likely that they were also aware that languages were written differently.

## Knowledge about written languages in the nursery

As soon as multilingual work in the nursery began, it became clear that some children had experience of different writing systems and could talk about this. Ace, aged 3, on only her third day in the nursery, walked confidently up to the table where some children were looking at food packets in different languages, and pointed to a Chinese drinks can, saying 'Why is this black Chinese writing here?' She had recognised the writing system and realised that it was unusual to find it in the classroom. The teacher and I asked her about Chinese writing at home, and she responded by telling us a story about hot soup falling on her head. When Ace's father came to collect her, he confirmed that the soup accident had happened several months earlier at a big family gathering for Chinese New Year.

So Ace could identify Chinese script, based on her home literacy experience, and she made a definite link between this script and the family setting in which it had been used. Shahina, a 5-year-old from a Bengali-speaking Muslim family who happened to be in the nursery that day, made a similar connection. Seeing the Arabic writing on a packet of curry powder, she observed 'That's from the Qur'an'. When I asked if she knew how to write like that, her answer was 'That's when we don't eat for a long time, then we can', referring to the fasting period of Ramadan and the feast of Eid. She went on to describe how her grandmother would read the Qur'an to her. In another conversation six months later, Shahina gave a lengthy explanation about Qur'anic literacy learning practices while showing me how she would write in Bengali and Arabic.

Shahina had longer experience of different scripts than 3-year-old Ace and could put her ideas into words more easily. But Ace's response indicated that she had the basis to develop ideas of this kind. It appeared that very young children could understand that different written languages existed. They could notice the types of symbols used and compare languages to each other.

Meera displayed this kind of bilingual understanding. Through her home experiences she had encountered two written languages, Gujarati and English. And as soon as she was given the chance, she was keen to use her knowledge about language at school. In this chapter I look at the many ways in which Meera, from the nursery to Year 2, investigated the Gujarati and English writing systems through texts which connected with her family and community life.

### 'I want my Gujarati'

At the age of three years and ten months, Meera was being taught by her parents to write in English, but not yet in Gujarati. But when her mother wrote in Gujarati for the display on 'Our Nursery Rules', Meera showed excitement and interest. She climbed up on a chair and added to this writing, using a thick felt-tip pen as her mother had done. For the rest of that school term she continued to add to the display, until the whole area next to her mother's writing was filled with Meera's 'Gujarati' in brightly-coloured felt-tip. As she wrote, Meera said 'I want my Gujarati' and 'I write like my mum'.

Meera was clearly aware that Gujarati existed as a separate written language and had a strong desire to write it herself. This awareness and desire in such a young child came as a surprise to us. From that first opportunity onwards, Meera continued to show interest in finding out more about Gujarati all through the school year. It was as if she had her own literacy agenda and was making use of the resources available to her to follow it through.

## Letters and numbers in Gujarati and English

At first, Meera's 'Gujarati' writing consisted of wavy lines. As well as writing on the 'Nursery Rules' display, she produced sheets of her own which she showed proudly to her mother and the nursery staff, saying 'That's Gujarati!' (see Fig.17). She referred to her mother's writing for help, saying for example 'I'm writing lots of Gujarati... I find something to do. Look at that', pointing to the display on the wall. Meanwhile, Meera could already write her own name in English, and was beginning to develop letters from her sister's name, also in English.

Later in that first term, Meera wrote some Gujarati alphabet letters with her mother in school, when parents and children were making cards together for the nursery 'postbox'. Meera's mother guided her hand to copy 'Meera' onto a card in Gujarati, and also wrote 'Pinal' (her sister's name) in Gujarati. Later, Meera wrote some symbols on another card and said 'It's Gujarati – Pinu my sister'. The symbols were complex and looked like emergent Gujarati (see Fig.18).

This 'Gujarati' writing was going on alongside English. Meera wrote several English alphabet letters, including some from Pinal's name, on one of the envelopes for her cards. So she was learning about the form of Gujarati and English script together, helped by her mother being an active writer in the nursery.

**55**

Meera's exploration of the different alphabetic systems continued during the second term. She knew that I brought some Gujarati alphabet and number teaching books to school and would often ask to look at them. One day she took the whole collection outside at playtime and sat in the climbing frame, which was structured like a little house, reading each book from cover to

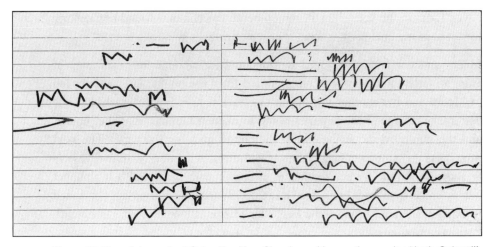

*Figure 17: Meera's 'wavy-line' Gujarati writing. She showed her mother, saying 'that's Gujarati!'*

*Figure 18: Card written by Meera: 'It's Gujarati – Pinu my sister' (above)*
*Compare with her name in English, written on the same day (below)*

cover. Later in the year she still remembered the books. I found her looking for them in my backpack, asking 'Did you bring some books today?'

Meera and her friends enjoyed writing on sheets containing examples of Gujarati letters and numbers, photocopied from the books. This activity led to Meera and her mother writing in Gujarati at home. Meera asked if she could take a large sheet of paper home to make a Gujarati alphabet poster, and she reminded me at the end of the day to give her the paper. The next time I was due at the nursery, Meera was waiting at the door with two posters to show me, made by her mother in Gujarati, with some English alphabet letters added by Meera herself. Meera's ability to write in English continued to expand; she could soon write her sister's name 'PINAL' in full, along with a variety of other letters.

The children could look at number systems in the nursery through calendars in different languages. Meera and her mother brought a Hindu religious calendar with 'English numbers' (Arabic numerals) and a Gujarati calendar. Using these for reference, Meera and her classmates made their own calendars with English and Gujarati numbers. Meera was particularly interested in the Gujarati numbers 'ek' (one) and 'chaar' (four, which was her age at the time).

Meera's learning about numbers was supported by home corner play. She and Colin frequently played a game Meera called 'Thomas Cook'. She had the idea that this was a shop where you could get money (as well as 'sweets and pineapple cake') and she would write numbers on small pieces of paper, such as a '2' which she called 'two pounds'. Other prices she mentioned were '1p' and '£4.50'. Her knowledge about numbers and prices drew on her experiences in the family shop. When the National Lottery began that year and tickets were sold in small shops such as her family's, Meera immediately offered me a 'lottery ticket' as part of her play, explaining 'You win £40'.

## A bilingual literacy repertoire

The alphabet and number work Meera did in the second term was brought together when she made a poster-sized text that included most of her current literacy repertoire. She began by announcing that she wanted to do something in Gujarati and after some thought decided 'I going to do numbers'. She went on to say 'I know how to do ABC', and this seemed to refer to English numbers, since she wrote a line of these from 1 to 12 along the top of the paper. She then said 'Where's that book?' and fetched the Gujarati numbers book.

Meera went on to cover the rest of the paper with a great variety of symbols and drawings. First came 'ABDDD PINAL' , which she said was 'my birthday' and 'my sister's name'. 'ABDDD' did contain some of the letters from 'BIRTHDAY'. Then she wrote symbols that looked like 'chaar' (the Gujarati 4), and 'ek' (the Gujarati 1), without looking at the Gujarati book. Later, she pointed out these numbers to me in the book. Next, she experimented with different ways of writing 'chaar', the number representing her age (4). She went on to write her own name and her sister's again in English. Then she added more numbers in English – her age, '4', and her sister's, '10' – along with various symbols which looked like emergent Gujarati. Meera linked her poster visually with home by including drawings of 'the daddy, the mummy, the door, the box, the steps and the bed'.

In her poster, Meera had combined her knowledge of numbers and letters in English and in Gujarati. She wanted to use these to represent ideas which were of personal importance to her, such as her own and her sister's names and ages, and the word 'birthday'. The concept of '4', her age, was repeated in both number systems. Again, Meera continued her literacy explorations at home. One day she brought to school a home-made card game in which one card contained English and Gujarati numbers, apparently written by a visiting friend, to which Meera had added more 'chaar' (4) symbols. When showing me the cards, Meera commented '1,2,3...Gujarati' (see Fig.19).

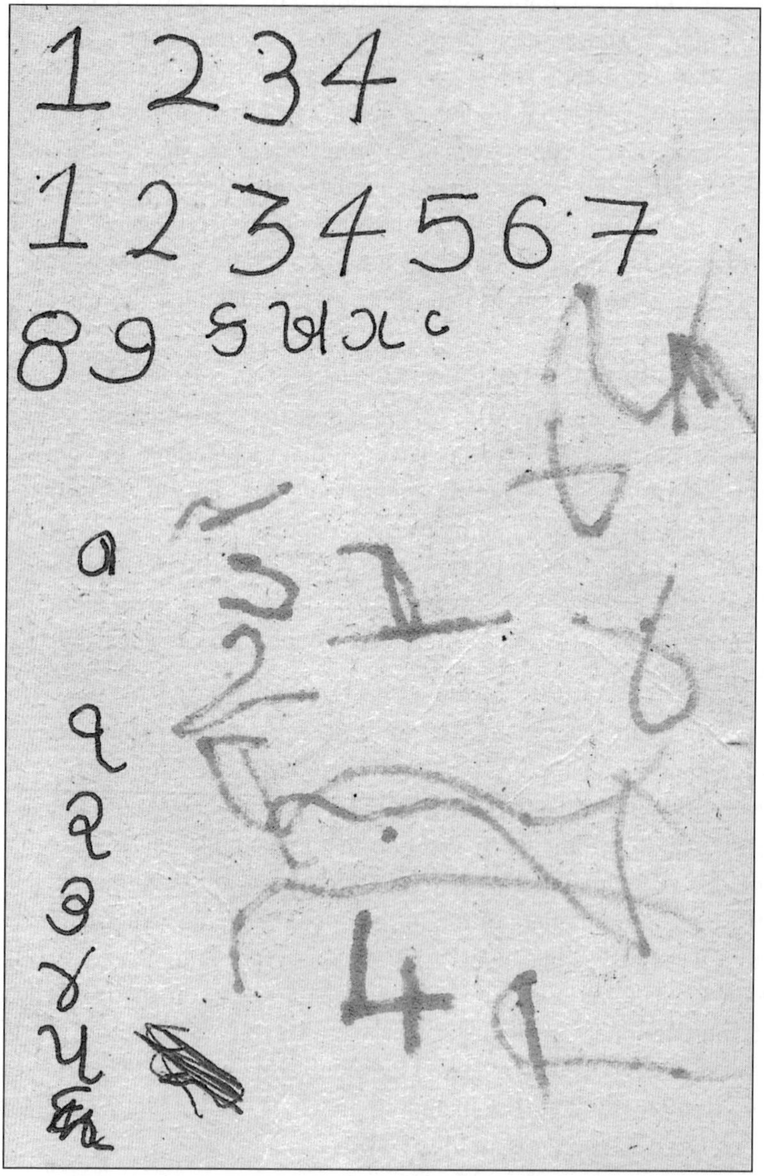

58

Figure 19: From a card game made by Meera at home with a friend: English and Gujarati numbers. Meera has experimented with 4 and its Gujarati equivalent

## Comparing languages: Meera's video posters

One of the most important home literacy materials for Meera was her video of an Indian film, 'Nashib'. She had started talking about 'films' and 'TV' at the very beginning of the research project, when she was putting her own 'Gujarati' writing next to her mother's. We became aware of the place Indian films held in Meera's family life, and suggested that she could bring one of her favourite films to school. The class watched an excerpt which Meera particularly liked, of singing and dancing followed by comedy. This was very popular with the children and a second showing was arranged.

We asked Meera's mother if she could make a poster showing the film title, which she did, sitting at the writing table in the nursery with Meera beside her. The poster included the film title and the names of Meera's favourite characters in both Gujarati and English, and was displayed on the nursery wall (see Fig.20).

On the same day, Meera began the first of several texts based on the poster. She decided to send a message about the video to her father. She asked me to draw her dad, which I did to the best of my limited ability (having met him once), and added her own drawing of her mum. Then, with encouragement, she produced a version of several of the Gujarati and English letters her mother had written (see Fig.21). She copied 'Nashib' in both languages and wrote the first part of her favourite character's name, 'Johan'. This was a difficult literacy challenge, particularly in Gujarati, and since this was Meera's first attempt her letters were schematic rather than detailed. As she finished,

**59**

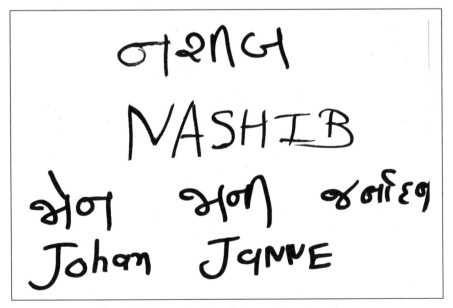

*Figure 20: Poster about film 'Nashib' by Meera's mother*

*Figure 21: Meera's message to her father about the video*

Meera said proudly 'I'm doing this! I could do this!' The video poster provided a powerful stimulus for writing because it had been made by her mother and because it was connected with the film 'Nashib', a highly significant home text.

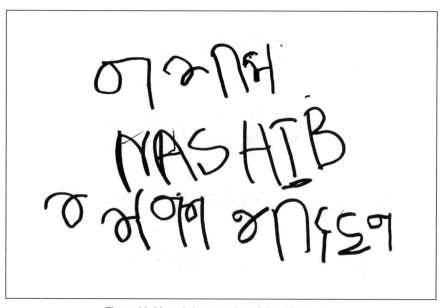

*Figure 22: Meera's later version of the video poster*

Over the next three months, Meera made four more video posters of her own. She was like a painter who returns to the same subject over and over again, treating it slightly differently each time and gaining new insight on each occasion. I thought of these posters as 'Meera's video series'. It was definitely a self-motivated project; she would say 'Where's my mum's video?' and 'I want to write my video'. She would ask for 'thick paper' and a big felt-tip pen, like the materials her mother had used.

The Gujarati symbols she produced, using her mother's writing as a model, became clearer and more detailed each time (see Fig.22). As she wrote, Meera made a running commentary on her task, either in conversation with me or as a monologue to herself. Her talk showed how she was thinking through ideas about written language. Some of these ideas were about the visual detail of Gujarati and English letters. She considered the handwriting sequence for Gujarati symbols, asking herself as she wrote a letter for the second time 'Did I do the line first? Yes I did do the line first'. She noticed that her mother's way of writing 'a' in English looked a bit like 'p', commenting 'My mummy done a 'p'. Never mind'.

Meera was also working on the idea of what the symbols in each language might represent. For example, she observed that a particular Gujarati letter was repeated and asked 'Why two of those?' She was interested in the English version of the names of characters in the film, 'Johan Janne', asking me persistently 'Why two J's?'

Another issue was how the symbols were organised on the page, and what this might mean. Although Meera did not yet refer to 'words', she noticed that symbols were grouped together with spaces between them and understood that these spaces must have significance, asking 'Why Mummy done a gap?' She also realised that each line of Gujarati script had an equivalent line in English written below. In one case there were three groupings of Gujarati letters and only two in English below, and Meera pointed this out, demanding 'Why three?' (It turned out that her mother had not been sure how to write the last word in English!) By making this comparison Meera showed that she knew the same concept was being represented in two different languages.

While working on her posters, Meera made remarks about the video as part of her family life: exactly where it was kept at home, whether she was allowed to put videos in the machine herself, who had or had not watched the film on Saturday. So her investigation of writing as a system was interwoven with her feelings about the social significance of the text – a video which, according to her father, Meera had watched many times when she was little, and which was typical of the films the family would watch together.

**61**

## The travel brochure: adult models and emergent writing

The pages made by Meera and her mother for the nursery's 'travel brochure' gave Meera another opportunity to write in both Gujarati and English. Several of the bilingual children and parents produced pages about the countries from which their families came. In Meera's case, she knew that in the approaching summer holidays she would be going to India to visit her grandparents – the recipients of the letters her mother wrote in Gujarati. So Meera was ready to contribute to the making of pages about India.

One day Meera announced that she wanted to do something in the home corner 'travel agency'. When I suggested the topic of India, she at once asked 'How do you write India?' Using my writing as a model, she put this word at the top of a sheet of paper. I asked 'What else would you like to do about India?' and she responded by writing a letter from the Gujarati alphabet. This was the first letter on her mother's video poster, and she did it from memory. The idea of writing about India had reminded her of a previous powerful model for Gujarati script.

Meera was concerned to get the handwriting sequence for this Gujarati symbol correct and asked me 'Does it go this way?' Then she wrote another symbol which looked visually like Gujarati script, although it was not recognisable as a particular letter. About this, Meera said 'Gujarati'. She followed with five more symbols that were unlike the English alphabet (of which Meera had a good command by this time) and seemed to be emergent Gujarati (see Fig.23). So in the first lines of her travel brochure page, Meera drew on adult models for particular Gujarati and English letters, and also did her own experimental writing. She wanted to use both these approaches to literacy learning.

## Interpreting graphic information

That afternoon Meera looked at a real travel brochure in the nursery and picked out the word 'India' from the list of countries advertised on the cover. She also found 'India' in the index and looked up the information on page 52. Sure enough, there was a map, and Meera read the word 'India' printed across it. The photos of India included street scenes with film posters displayed on advertising hoardings. Meera recognised these and commented on them: 'I want to see a film... I like this film... we watch that one'. She cut out a picture of the Taj Mahal with caption, to stick underneath the writing of 'India' and the 'Gujarati' she had done earlier. We also looked through a table of dates and prices for holidays in India.

Thus Meera's cultural knowledge and her interest in India led her to engage with different aspects of literacy through the travel brochure text: identifying words and numbers, using an index, interpreting photographs and maps, and thinking about dates and prices. When her mother arrived she reinforced this learning by pointing out on the map the area where her grandparents lived, in Gujarat in northwest India, and we discussed how much the plane ticket cost – Meera's mother said £500.

*Figure 23: Meera's first travel brochure page (with later additions)*

## Key words and numbers

Two days later Meera was keen to continue writing about this aspect of her life. She said 'Can I write some India – I need some India'. She wanted to do 'a big India – so everyone can see' and made a poster by writing letter strings which began 'ANi' which she put up on the home corner wall. She began a new page for the travel brochure, with her own writing of 'INDDIA' at the top. This had become a key word for her to work on in her literacy learning.

Meera also tackled the word 'Gujarat' in Gujarati for her new brochure page. When she cut out the map of India we had been studying and stuck it centrally on the page, we discussed again where her grandparents lived and I suggested writing 'Gujarat' next to that part of the map. Meera was able to refer to her mother's writing of 'Gujarat' in Gujarati and English, which she had left with us on her most recent visit. Meera wrote each letter of the word down the side of the map, commenting that one letter was 'chaar' (it did indeed look like the Gujarati symbol for '4') and saying 'I can do that one' because she had written it many times before. She then wrote a string of English letters underneath the map and said 'That's Gujarat'. Although she had not used the correct English letters, her aim was clear – to provide two versions of the word 'Gujarat' on her brochure page, one in each language (see Fig.24).

64

Meera continued her literacy work in English by confidently writing 'Taj Mahal' from my model, to caption a picture of the famous monument which her mother had brought from home. Meera was particularly interested in the 'M' and we talked about its sound, and the names of her friends in the nursery beginning with 'M'. She asked if I had an 'M' and I wrote my name to show her that I did. We also added the price of an air ticket to India, £500, to her original brochure page, which involved Meera working out how to write the number 500 and the pound sign with my help.

## Thinking through ideas about writing

Three weeks later, having engaged in many other literacy activities meanwhile, Meera returned to the 'travel brochure' pages, showing that they represented something important to her home life and that she had been thinking about the ideas involved. She picked out her first page with 'India' and the cutting of the Taj Mahal, then said 'I want to write my Gujarati'. She added another Gujarati letter to the page – again, this was the first letter from the video poster – and commented 'Haven't watched my video for too long'. The meaning of this symbol and its connection with Gujarati writing and with India was constantly on her mind.

*Figure 24: Meera's second travel brochure page*

While she was looking at this page, Meera remembered the significance of '£500' and asked 'How much India cost?' Finally, she wrote 'AB4' underneath, probably to represent her favourite concepts of 'BIRTHDAY' and her age. She asked me my age and added it, followed by the age of her classmate Ace who was with us at the time. She asked me my sister's age and put that in too. As well as exploring further ideas about numbers, it was as if she were adding some personal details about the people involved in the writing activity, almost like a 'signature' to finish the page.

Her work on the travel brochure required Meera to write in English and Gujarati, both from adult examples (my writing of 'INDIA' and her mother's of 'Gujarat') and her own emergent versions (her English letter string for 'Gujarat', and the varied symbols which she called 'Gujarati'). Her 'brochure pages' were bilingual texts, like most of the others I saw her write spontaneously towards the end of the school year. As she produced texts in English which were becoming lengthier and more complex, Meera incorporated the Gujarati symbols which she was in the process of defining for herself.

## Ages 5 and 6: maintaining biliteracy connections

In the next two school years of Reception and Year 1, as Meera turned 5 and then 6 years old, she continued to be enthusiastic about the opportunity to write Gujarati in school. She and her mother brought Gujarati newspapers to the family Language Workshops (described earlier) and Meera made her own newspapers with her mother's help. These consisted of large sheets of folded paper on which she stuck cuttings of her choice and added drawings and writing. In this literacy activity, Meera again showed her desire to represent the important ideas and events in her social and cultural life. She was still very interested in Indian films and included advertisements for several in her newspaper, writing the titles (such as 'Daraar video') below her cuttings. She also picked out advertisements with photographs of decorated 'mandaps' for weddings and wrote 'wedding' underneath them.

The newspapers were written bilingually in English and Gujarati and Meera used English writing for her film and wedding captions. She cut out a crossword and wordsearch in Gujarati and wanted to make a wordsearch of her own, similar to those she had often seen her mother doing at home. To help in the production of this wordsearch, Meera's mother sat beside her in the classroom, encouraging her to write letters and numbers in Gujarati.

## Age 7: a Gujarati wordsearch

By age 7 Meera was in Year 2 and was writing confidently in English. She had continued to see her mother writing letters to India in Gujarati and doing wordsearches from the newspaper, although she was not yet being formally taught to write in Gujarati. When multilingual activities were offered in school, Meera began to apply her knowledge about the English writing system to Gujarati in new and unexpected ways.

One of the class topics in Year 2 was 'animals'. As part of their work, children were drawing and writing about an animal of their choice, using information books available in the classroom. The teacher and I agreed that weekly sessions of multilingual work could be done around this topic and sent home to parents a sheet listing animal names and asking for help with translation. Families were keen to help and the children brought back the sheets in several languages, including Gujarati, Chinese and Thai. The children and I also consulted bilingual dictionaries available in school to find the words we needed. After the whole class had taken it in turns to participate in the sessions, we produced a display about animals in different languages. This was put up in the school corridor and showed the children's writing of the names of the animals, accompanied by their drawings.

Meera's mother was one of the parents who provided translations of the list of animal names, and her Gujarati writing was referred to by Meera and other children when making items for the display. Meera and her mother also produced a wordsearch in Gujarati for the 'animals' topic, which they brought to school. It was extensive and included many animal names. The teacher and I were very impressed, and at our request Meera took it home and made a larger version for the display. She wrote a separate list of animal names to look for in the wordsearch. 'Elephant', 'fox', 'horse' and others were written in Gujarati with the English translation alongside. Meera also provided instructions, which were as follows:

*The word search is about language in Gujarati.*
*The words are animals words in Gujarati.*
*The rules are*
*no cheating*
*dont circle around any old word*
*dont write over the words in pen.*

Meera was proud to see her Gujarati writing being displayed in the school corridor, and her instructions show that she had a feeling of confident ownership towards the material.

### 'I can write every single word in Gujarati'

Making this wordsearch seemed to act as another catalyst for Meera's involvement with Gujarati writing. She told me 'I wrote the Gujarati alphabet with my mum – she showed me for the wordsearch. I didn't know before'. She began to talk confidently about her knowledge of Gujarati, making

**67**

remarks such as 'I know animals in Gujarati' and 'Some letters aren't in the Gujarati alphabet, like H'. And once she stated 'I can write every single word in Gujarati'.

I was curious to find out more about Meera's ideas. I arranged to talk to her one lunchtime about reading and writing in Gujarati, and during this interview I asked her if she could write some words for me in Gujarati. Meera was delighted to do so, and decided to write animal names (see Fig.25). The first word she wrote appears on the second line, and she said it was 'fox'. Her comment was 'it's supposed to be like that because O and X don't have a meaning' (I presumed she meant that these letters did not exist in Gujarati). Next she said 'I can do frog', 'I can write elephant'. She put these underneath 'fox' (lines 3 and 4 in the figure). Then she said 'I can write the numbers. Shall I write thousand?' She did this above (on the first line).

The words 'fox' and 'frog' look very like their English equivalents. I began to wonder whether Meera was transliterating English words into Gujarati. And perhaps where there were no equivalent letters in Gujarati, as she thought was true of O and X, she was using English ones. If this was the case, I wondered how accurate her knowledge of Gujarati letters was. If there were any she did not know, was she inventing symbols at random?

68 Although I had gained some knowledge about Gujarati script over the years, I needed help to interpret Meera's writing. Meera's mother was rarely in school at this time because of home commitments, so I sought advice from another adult who was literate in Gujarati.

## Meera's 'Gujarati' code

It turned out that Meera's writing could be read by someone well versed in Gujarati script. She was indeed transliterating, using Gujarati letters which she thought had similar sounds to those of each English letter (see Fig.26). For example, her first word was meant to be read out as 'f-r-o-g' rather than the

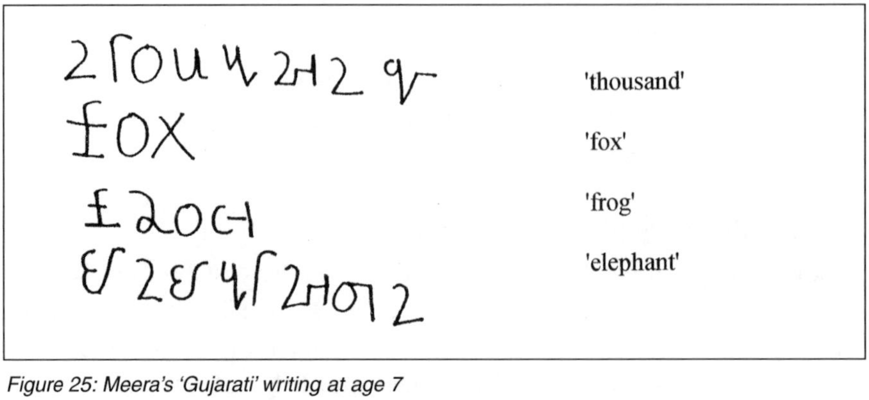

Figure 25: Meera's 'Gujarati' writing at age 7

Gujarati word for frog. This was in line with the idea I had seen Meera's mother use with her in the Year 1 newspaper workshop, where she wrote the English alphabet sequence and put alongside each letter a Gujarati symbol which sounded similar. I also remembered Meera's mother showing her the Gujarati letters which produced sounds such as /m/ and /r/ when writing 'Meera'. There is no exact equivalence between letters in the two languages, since Gujarati is written syllabically whereas English is alphabetic and many English letters can have several different sounds. However, this approach can be used quite successfully to represent English words via Gujarati symbols.

Meera had taken up this idea in order to write 'every single word' in Gujarati. Drawing on her knowledge of how written language works in English, she had made use of the phonetic principle and tried to create sound-symbol correspondence. Although she did not necessarily know the words for 'frog' or 'fox' in Gujarati, she had found a way of getting round this problem by representing the English words in Gujarati script.

When I looked closely at how Meera had transliterated English words into 'Gujarati' (see figure) I could see that she had taken a logical approach to her task. She was familiar with a number of Gujarati letters and could write them recognisably (such as those which sounded similar to A, E, F, L, N, P, and R). Her use of these letters to transliterate was largely correct, although some-times she wrote a letter accurately but put it in the wrong place (so 'frog' reads as 'frol'). She was right in thinking that there was no 'X' in Gujarati, so she used an English one. As I mentioned earlier, she had told me there was no 'H' in Gujarati, so she seemed to have invented her own, which looks more like Gujarati script than English, and which she used with consistency. She also seemed to have invented a symbol for 'T': this looks similar to the Gujarati number 2, which Meera had studied in the past. Again, she was con-sistent about using it.

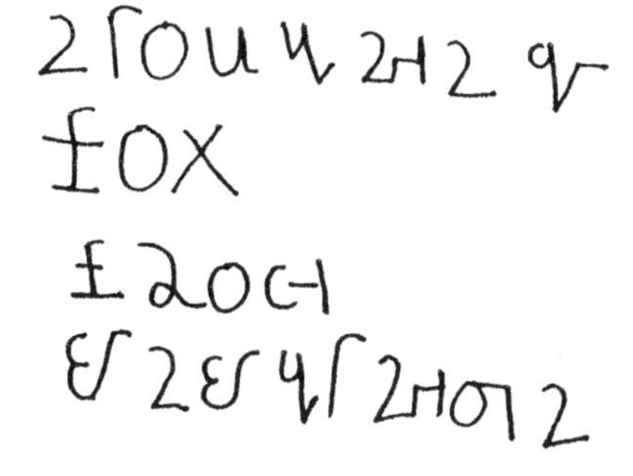

**69**

(T) (H) <u>O</u> <u>U</u> P A (T) ?

F <u>O</u> X

F R <u>O</u> L

E (T) E P (H) A N (T)

*Figure 26: A transliteration of Meera's 'Gujarati' writing*

So Meera was operating according to a system of her own, a code based on a combination of her knowledge of the English and Gujarati alphabets. When I went back to the wordsearch she had made for the display at school, I found she had used her own system there too. Although the separate list of animals to look for was in 'real' Gujarati, probably based on her mother's writing, the actual wordsearch was in Meera's Gujarati. In fact, she had written a completely new list of animals to look for directly underneath the grid, in her own code, which I could now decipher: it said, as far as I could tell, 'elephant, fox, penguin, hamster, pony, horse, frog, cat'. Meera had carefully placed a vertical line between each word to separate it from the next one. As well as some animals from her original list, she had included new ones which she was personally interested in. For example, 'penguin' – the animal she'd chosen to do research on for her topic work at school, and 'hamster' – she had a hamster as a pet. Sure enough, when I looked for these words in the wordsearch I found every one, carefully concealed amongst other 'Gujarati' letters.

What Meera said about making this wordsearch was 'My mum wrote down some letters and I copied them. Next day I finished it because I remembered the letters'.

So 'remembering the letters' involved using the knowledge she had gained about Gujarati script in her own way. Although Meera was not writing 'correctly', her work was an impressive feat. It showed the complexity of her thinking about written language and her continuing desire to investigate both literacies simultaneously. As well as drawing on her knowledge of how the phonetic principle works in English, she had used her knowledge of Gujarati letters, both in terms of the general appearance of the script compared to English and of particular symbols which she had seen in her mother's writing and other Gujarati texts.

## Linking home and school identities

Once again Meera's literacy work was based on a text from home – the Gujarati wordsearches which she had observed her mother doing since she was very young. Meera went on to adapt this idea to another topic area which she wanted to write about. During our conversation about reading and writing in Gujarati at home, she emphasised her enjoyment of making wordsearches, and surprised me by stating that she hoped to make one about football, because 'I support Arsenal'.

I later discovered that Meera was very knowledgeable about football; she regularly made remarks to me about Arsenal's matches and about the World Cup that summer. Being a football fan was part of her peer group identity at

70

school. Girls as well as boys talked about football together, and Meera was in a playground 'club' called 'The Football Fever Club'. According to the membership list Ace showed to me, the club consisted of three boys as 'members', while Meera and Ace were 'owners'.

By making a wordsearch in Gujarati about Arsenal, Meera could unite her home and school worlds. This gave her another strong reason for writing Gujarati letters and continuing to explore their relationship to English letters. Soon afterwards, Meera brought her Arsenal wordsearch into school to show me. It was another large and complex document, consisting of a 15 by 15 square grid filled with symbols from Meera's Gujarati code – 225 letters altogether (see Fig.27). Meera explained that the words to look for were the following names of footballers: Petit, Bergkamp, Ankella (she probably meant Anelka), Dixon and Seaman. The words she had written underneath the grid, when read using her code, actually seemed to say Pett (Petit?) Deacs (Dixon?) Adam (probably Tony Adams, the Arsenal captain), Patreb (possibly Patrick Vieira), and Thermamp (presumably Bergkamp), all currently members of the Arsenal team. My transliteration is given underneath Meera's text. The amount of detail in this wordsearch is striking, and it is possible to find within the grid all the names written below.

For Meera, the production of the Arsenal wordsearch in Gujarati was partly a way of investigating languages and partly an avenue through which she could express and construct her linguistic and cultural identity. As a 7-year-old girl of South Asian origin growing up in London, this identity was already very complex. The Indian films she watched were in several languages including English, her favourite film stars wore baseball caps and jeans, and the songs from the films (which she loved to sing along with and dance to) were a complete musical mixture, from bhangra to 70's reggae. She also told me that her cousin had insisted that she did a dance to a Spice Girls number at his wedding. So it's not surprising that she wanted to create a new kind of text, still based on her mother's use of Gujarati at home, but moving into areas of bilingual youth culture.

71

Meera did not find it difficult to unite her two languages and her home and school worlds. Whenever given the opportunity, she was eager to do so and took advantage of it to compare and investigate the English and Gujarati writing systems. As she reacted excitedly to seeing her mother's Gujarati writing on the nursery wall and produced her own video posters and newspapers in both languages, the teachers and I felt that she had become a writer whose literacy learning drew on the full range of her cultural resources.

**72**

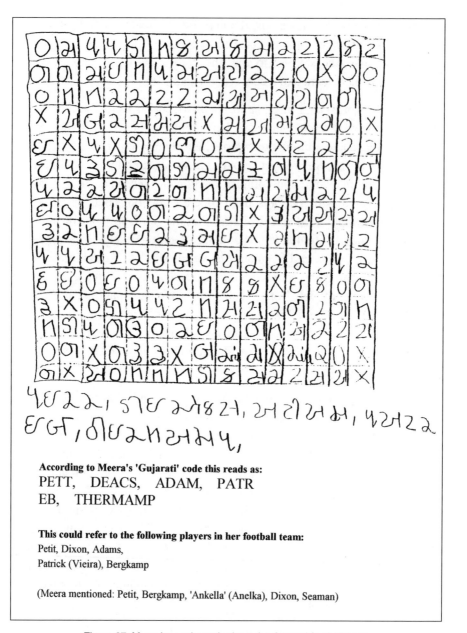

**According to Meera's 'Gujarati' code this reads as:**

PETT,   DEACS,   ADAM,   PATR
EB,   THERMAMP

**This could refer to the following players in her football team:**
Petit, Dixon, Adams,
Patrick (Vieira), Bergkamp

(Meera mentioned: Petit, Bergkamp, 'Ankella' (Anelka), Dixon, Seaman)

*Figure 27: Meera's wordsearch about the Arsenal football team*

## Ideas for helping children to investigate written languages

- Even if children are not yet being taught to write in their mother tongue at home, they may – like Meera – have a desire to explore the written language and school can give them this opportunity. In their classroom learning, they will then be able to draw on their observations of how different writing systems are used in everyday literacy events.

- Multilingual literacy work in the classroom can provide a reason for parents and children to write together at home as well as at school. If families begin to help with making alphabet posters and calendars, translating material for classroom study and writing cards and letters, these activities are likely to be partly completed at home. This can stimulate further dialogue between parents and children about how different writing systems work.

- Teachers can offer bilingual children the chance to assume the role of 'expert' on how to read and write their home languages. Children can find out more and help the teacher and their classmates to learn about the language. Some children, like Meera, may take this on as a 'project' to actively pursue.

- When children are making multilingual texts at school, they are likely to comment on differences and similarities they observe between languages. If teachers can 'listen in' on these monologues and conversations, they will gain insight into children's ideas about English writing as well as other writing systems. The children's comments can be built on later in whole-class discussion.

- Many texts which children see used at home are bilingual (e.g. newspapers in different languages often contain some English). Texts written by parents in the classroom will usually be bilingual too (e.g. the video poster made by Meera's mother). Meera used bilingual texts to compare languages, and teachers can encourage these comparisons. For example:

  - Children can identify the visual differences between each language (they will tune into the smallest details – even if a language has a similar script to English, such as Turkish or Spanish, they will find the different accents which characterise it). As well as helping children with first language literacy, this also highlights the characteristics of English script.

  - Children can work out whether languages are written from right to left, left to right, vertically or horizontally. Young children are perfectly capable of coping with different directionalities – this is the kind of thing they are in the process of investigating as they discover

**73**

how literacies work. Explicit discussion of these differences helps to clarify their ideas.

- Children can compare equivalent words and phrases. How are they grouped together? Do they have the same number of letters/symbols? (You don't have to be an expert on different languages to help children do this! The very process of thinking through the issues clarifies concepts such as 'letter', 'word' and 'sentence'. Questions can be raised which parents and others can help to answer later.)

• You can encourage children to put on paper all the letters and numbers they know in different languages (their own languages and others available in the classroom) – like Meera's poster in which she wrote her current repertoire. Children also like to fill in empty grids (which look like alphabet posters or calendars) with symbols which interest them, including invented ones they are experimenting with. These activities help children to rehearse and expand their literacy repertoires.

• Children can make card games and wordsearches like Meera's, which involve finding and matching words and letters in different languages. These can be done at school or home and the making will give rise to discussion about the meaning of different symbols.

**74**   • Computer software packages are available in different fonts and these can be made available to parents and children in school. They can be enormously useful in helping adult and child literacy, since symbols can be quickly produced and recognised. The work of Urmi Chana, Viv Edwards and Sue Walker (1997) provides ideas on using multilingual software in schools.

# CHAPTER FIVE

# Mohammed:
# Designing Different Texts

For bilingual children learning about literacy, there are a great many different kinds of symbol to attend to. As well as learning two languages which may have quite different scripts, they notice that pictures, diagrams, logos and other graphic symbols are used to represent ideas in the world around them. The children making 'travel brochure' pages in the nursery, for example, showed they knew that visual images could be combined with writing to convey meaning. Billy and Meera put maps of Thailand and India centrally on their pages. Ace chose photos of a skyscraper and a stylish young woman to represent Hong Kong. Around these images the children wrote, using symbols which stood for messages about themselves and the countries their families came from. The visual arrangement of the text was not accidental – children made decisions about where to place the pictures and where to write.

The recent work of Gunther Kress (1997) suggests that children are acting appropriately by paying attention to these different ways of making meaning. The visual features of a text have always been important (a report looks very different from a formal letter or a poem, for example, and the choice of font gives a particular impression – of tradition, of modernity, of warmth and informality – as does the size, colour and texture of paper chosen). But nowadays the visual aspect is even more significant; relatively few texts contain words alone. Most use diagrams, pictures or other graphic symbols to put across ideas as well.

In order to be able to design texts like these in the future, children need to learn how to create them. Their home lives give them plenty of experience of 'multi-modal' texts which combine words and images with speech and music: television, video, CD Roms. A certain amount of their educational experience also involves such media, but when it comes to making their own texts the emphasis is usually on the written word: 'Do your writing first – you can draw a picture when you finish'. But for the child, the picture might be an integral part of the text, carrying important meanings. As part of literacy learning, teachers can give children opportunities to combine writing and visuals in their text-making, and discuss ways of doing so.

## A world of variety

Bilingual children with experience of different scripts have an extra reason for knowing that written messages can be expressed in different ways. They are in a good position to add a variety of symbols to their literacy repertoire and use them with flexibility in different types of text. This chapter relates how one particular child took this approach in the nursery.

Mohammed had grown up with three visually different scripts: Arabic, Gujarati and English. We noted in Chapter 2 that he could discriminate between them and that he quickly came to recognise other scripts he encountered, such as Chinese. He was very interested in images and logos, and often combined them with writing. By looking at texts Mohammed produced over a period of three months, we can see how he varied his choice of symbols according to the purpose he wanted to achieve.

## Writing for different purposes

When the research began, Mohammed was 4 years 8 months old and it was his last term in the nursery before moving into the main school. He enjoyed writing and was often to be found in the home corner or the writing area, joining in with role-plays and making his own texts. This connected with his mother's comments about Mohammed's activities at home: running his 'cafe' or 'school', sending letters to his cousin, drawing and writing about his father's car, adding his own writing to family letters in Gujarati.

During the term, Mohammed's texts were extremely varied and the way he used his writing and other symbols did not follow an obvious 'developmental sequence'. For example, within the first three weeks of the research he wrote his name fully in English above a drawing of his family, used 'wavy-line' writing to accompany pictures of food for a 'recipe', filled in a catalogue order form with a drawing of a whistle and 'wavy-line' writing, produced a strikingly detailed Arabic alphabet poster, and showed how he could write his friends' names 'Ace' and 'Tex'. As the term went on, he continued to produce this kind of variety.

Mohammed treated each of his texts in a very particular way. We focus on several of them in this chapter – the recipe, the order form, the Arabic alphabet poster and his texts about his father's car. By looking at what he was trying to convey in each case and the context in which he was writing, we can understand why they look so different. Each text played its part in his development of ideas about different symbols and how they could be used.

## Mohammed's recipe

The 'recipe' was produced while role-plays were going on around 'cooking' in the home corner. Children were busy putting papier-machè food items into plastic saucepans on the toy stove, stirring them and serving them to me and to each other. I asked if they could write a recipe for the dish they were making. Mohammed began not with writing but with drawings, of 'one apple, two oranges, cake with jelly'. He then explained to me how to make the dish. I said I might forget and asked if he could write the instructions down for me, whereupon he added several lines of 'wavy-line' writing above the pictures (see Fig.28).

Knowing that Mohammed could already write a number of alphabet letters, we might wonder why he did not use any in his recipe. This was probably

*Figure 28: Mohammed's recipe: 'one apple, two oranges, cake with jelly'*

77

because his main aim was to show the ingredients 'one apple, two oranges' visually, along with the finished dish 'cake with jelly'. When I talked with Mohammed's mother that afternoon she told me how much he loved cooking. He would watch cookery programmes on TV and come into the kitchen to tell her how to make a dish he had just seen being prepared. On TV the camera focuses on the ingredients in close-up, while cookery books show glossy pictures, and Mohammed seemed to be doing the same.

The writing of the instructions was less important for Mohammed, but he understood the idea and was prepared to do it when I asked. He covered the top part of the page with wavy lines, which look like lines of print set out in two columns, as in some recipe books. By writing this way, Mohammed could show me that he knew the layout of a recipe and could quickly 'act as a writer' in answer to my request. However, his main interest remained in the visuals; six weeks later he drew similar pictures again, with no writing, and told me 'This is the letter for a recipe... this is apple here, and this is orange.'

## Mohammed's catalogue order form

A week later, Mohammed and other children were gathered in the home corner, surrounded by catalogues for play equipment and a pad of old order forms from the school office. I asked if they would like to choose something for the nursery and use the order forms. The children understood this idea and began to fill in the forms. We knew from the parents that catalogue ordering was a popular activity at home. For example, Zubeadat saw order forms being filled in and would point to items in the catalogue, saying 'that's for me'. Adedamola would tell his mother 'I want you to buy this'. Michaela would fill in the order forms herself.

In the nursery activity, the children mostly used lines, dots or shapes which fitted into the boxes on the grid, showing that they knew what this layout required. Vanessa made marks in one column and said 'I want those'. Hamish filled in some boxes with crosses. Mohammed wrote free-flowing horizontal wavy lines across his form, and heavily circled the £ sign at the bottom of the price column. The children put their order forms in envelopes and when I asked Mohammed where he was sending his, he said 'to the shop'.

Colin, meanwhile, found a new angle. He started cutting out pictures of the items he wanted from the catalogues and putting them in his envelope. His classmates followed enthusiastically and this soon became the main focus of the activity. Even though several of the children knew some alphabet letters and could have written about the products they had chosen, the pictures were an excellent way of representing their order. Mohammed joined in immediately. He had decided to order a whistle, a flute and some keyrings. He also drew a picture on his order form which looked like a whistle.

The children understood the procedures involved in ordering, and their eventual goal. Colin went to tell Helen, his teacher, 'I've ordered something for you', and later told the whole class that 'the man will bring toys to the nursery', 'some scissors for you, Helen'. Mohammed repeated his intention of sending his order 'to the shop'. Their interest in the visuals showed that they knew this was a powerful way of expressing ideas (and indeed images are used more and more often to symbolise meaning in the world around us, such as the icons we now click on to operate computer software). The children's ability to 'fill in forms' also showed that they had been paying attention to the organisation of symbols such as ticks and crosses on a grid, as well as lines of writing.

These factors can explain why Mohammed's order form contained a picture of one of the items he wanted plus 'wavy lines' to stand for writing which filled up the grid. Mohammed's interest in order forms at home and at school continued. Later in the term he brought an order form and tokens from a cereal packet to show me, explaining that 'to get a toy' you had to 'cut out', 'write address' on the form, and 'send them'.

## Mohammed's Arabic alphabet poster

On the same day as the catalogue ordering activity, Mohammed and his mother brought into the nursery a tape of an Arabic alphabet song and the accompanying pack of flashcards. These were the materials they had been using together at home, as Mohammed's mother prepared him for the Qur'anic literacy classes which he was about to begin.

When Mohammed looked at the flashcards with a small group of classmates, it was evident that he was familiar with a number of the Arabic alphabet letters. He picked out the cards on which 'alif' and 'jeem' were written. He could identify these letters amongst the array of different ones shown on the cover card. And when I pointed to other letters on the cover card, he could find them among the individual cards, whereas his classmates found this difficult. Mohammed's ability to discriminate visually between the letters had been enhanced by his mother's teaching.

Mohammed's tape was a recording of the Arabic alphabet sung to music by a group of children. As described in Chapter 2, Helen and I used this tape with the whole class so that the nursery group could hear and see an alphabet different from English. Mohammed's mother made a large poster of the alphabet to help us all to sing along with the words of the song. The children enjoyed this activity and we repeated the listening and singing several times in that first session, with the poster held up prominently in front of the class.

As the session finished, I suggested that children might want to make another poster like this one later that day. That afternoon Mohammed came up to me at the writing table and stood there quietly. I asked if he wanted to make a poster and he nodded. Equipped with a large sheet of paper and a thick felt-tip pen, he began, using his mother's poster as a model. Writing from right to left, he did the first few letters with impressive accuracy but soon stopped in dissatisfaction, saying 'it doesn't look the same'. Without a grid to help him, his row of letters was wandering down the page. I asked if he wanted boxes like the ones on his mother's poster and he confirmed that he did.

When I drew a grid on the other side of the page, Mohammed began again and this time he completed the entire alphabet at one sitting (see Fig.29). He wrote each letter in order, with great concentration and attention to detail. He particularly enjoyed adding the dots that characterise some of the letters, with an emphatic flourish of his felt-tip pen. Helen and I were impressed by the length of time which Mohammed devoted to this activity and by the accuracy of the result. We assumed that Mohammed must have written the alphabet with his mother a number of times already.

However, when Mohammed's mother arrived that afternoon she was amazed. 'He's never written Arabic before!', she told us. Mohammed was being taught to read the alphabet at home but not yet to write it. Only then did we realise how closely he must have been paying attention to the script when he

**80**

Figure 29: Mohammed's Arabic alphabet poster

was studying the chart and flashcards with his mother. His investigation would have been fuelled by the significance of Qur'anic writing within his family, and the knowledge that his sister was already attending classes which he would soon join. These factors had motivated Mohammed to write the entire alphabet himself when the opportunity arose in the nursery. It was a demanding task for a 4 year old, but he also knew that his teacher and I would appreciate his work, because the Arabic alphabet poster had been given a high status in the classroom.

In his recipe and his order form, Mohammed's focus had been on the pictures of key items and the overall appearance of the text. In his alphabet poster, he was also concerned with the layout – he was dissatisfied when it did not at first resemble his mother's regular spacing – but he was particularly interested in the details of each individual letter. On this occasion he wanted to produce a complete, correct alphabet. And what is more, it was the Qur'anic alphabet. Mohammed may well have been aware that although emergent writing was accepted in his English nursery, recognisable letters would be required in his Qur'anic literacy class. So there was an extra reason for concentrating on the detail of the letters rather than on other aspects of his poster.

Several weeks later, after the whole class had listened to the Arabic alphabet tape again, I saw Mohammed sitting by himself, making another poster. When he had finished, he cut it up into separate squares and put them in his pocket to take home. These, presumably, were his own flashcards – and again, the individual letters were important for this purpose.

**81**

## Mohammed's 'car' texts

To Mohammed, his dad's car was something special and it was the centre-piece of many fascinating events. His mother told me how he would do drawings at home, showing her for example 'this is daddy changing the wheel'. One day Mohammed wrote the letters M O T in the nursery. They were in reverse order, T O M, with a circle round each letter to give them emphasis. He told me 'it's the station – fix the car – in Leicester'. His mother confirmed that he had indeed accompanied his dad to take the car for its annual MOT safety check when they were visiting family in Leicester. But this had happened several months ago and she was surprised that he remembered the lettering from the MOT sign.

For Mohammed, however, the symbols MOT represented a highly significant experience. He described to me at length what had happened during the MOT check and was particularly enthusiastic about how the car was levered into the air on the automatic ramp: 'it was going up and down... and when you come back it'd go up up up and down'. These exciting events, linked with the three-letter acronym, had remained in his memory and he was still thinking about their meaning.

Mohammed's drawings of cars continued. Two weeks after his MOT texts, he drew a car beside a set of traffic lights and wrote his name above the pictures. On the same day he began to use another piece of writing that fascinated him: the slogan 'I ❤ U'. He told me 'my cousin wrote it on my hand' (and Mohammed's mother later reported that he had recently seen a birthday card to her from his sister that bore the same message). On this day Mohammed wrote one text with 'I ❤ U', did one drawing of his dad's car by itself, and produced another text with 'I ❤ U' next to a picture of a car (see Fig.30).

Mohammed was exploring the idea of combining symbolic messages. It seems likely that he knew 'I ❤ U' said something about relationships between people who loved each other. Given his attachment to his dad's car, it is quite possible that he wanted to make a statement about his feelings for this 'love object'. In the nursery on that same day, he produced another text which goes even further, combining the car and 'I ❤ U' with more written messages (see Fig.31).

Here the car is the central image, which shows its prime importance for Mohammed. It is drawn in detail, complete with windows, steering wheel and a handle to open the boot. The picture is framed by a variety of writing. Mohammed's name is at the top, showing him to be the author and connecting him with the messages below. 'I ❤ U' appears twice – at the front of the car and again behind it. Other hearts surround the car, reinforcing the 'love' message.

Directly above the car Mohammed has written his version of the word 'Nissan'. This brand name was highly significant to him; it characterised the car. When I asked him 'Do you like your dad's car?' he replied simply 'it's a Nissan'. His text, showing the image of the car prominently with the brand

**82**

Figure 30: Mohammed's 'I❤U' plus car

*Figure 31: Mohammed's 'car' text*

name, is rather like the advertisements he would have seen on street hoardings and TV.

Knowing Mohammed's current interests, Helen and I were struck by the way in which he had managed to combine them into one complex text. Helen commented 'it's like a cross-section of a person's thoughts'. The text is also an opportunity for Mohammed to rehearse part of his literacy repertoire, as Meera did in the poster described in Chapter 4. He has placed 'ABC' as part of the framing of the car, the letters that were often used by the nursery children to symbolise the alphabet and their knowledge of it.

## Developing key symbols

Mohammed focused his explorations of literacy on the words and other symbols which held particular meaning for him. He was currently developing his writing of a number of alphabet letters and the word 'Nissan' was involved, along with the names of people who were important to him. He wrote 'Nissan' in his car text as 'AinSS' without adult help, indicating that he had been studying the name. One week later, he drew another picture of a car and traffic lights and asked me to write 'Nissan' beside the drawings. The following day he drew a circular car badge divided into two halves by a horizontal line. He asked me to write 'Nissan' in the top section and 'Stanza' in the bottom section. At first I did not understand the word 'Stanza', so he clarified his request: 'Nissan Stanza – my dad's car'. He wanted me to help him build up his knowledge of these words.

The word 'Nissan' happened to have some letters in common with the name of Mohammed's mother, Aisha, and with my name, Charmian. All three words contain 'A' and 'I', and two out of three share 'N' and 'S'. Mohammed began to develop these letters quite quickly. When writing letters for the nursery's Christmas 'postbox', he put NHAAiA on an envelope and said this was 'Charmian'. Sure enough, I appeared on the 'stamp' too – he drew a picture of me in a square outlined in one corner of the envelope (see Fig.32). The letter inside said AiAHNi. He then wrote 'Ai' for his mother's name and asked me to complete it. The next time he wrote 'AiS' and asked me to write the rest. Other letters he wrote for me that day were addressed to 'NAiN' and 'NAiT'.

## Making use of different symbols

Throughout the term, Mohammed was continually working on his knowledge of the English and Arabic alphabets. At the same time, he took much interest in other aspects of text, such as how writing was combined with visuals. For example, in his letter to me he used two ways of representing me symbolically – by writing my name and by drawing me on the 'stamp'. He had noted the way symbols were organised on envelopes and incorporated this into his own design. His stamp was in the corner of the envelope but my written name was placed more centrally.

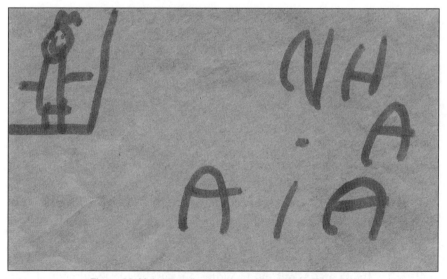

*Figure 32: Mohammed's envelope addressed to Charmian.*
*Charmian also appears on the stamp*

Mohammed was also interested in other written symbols which were not part of the alphabets he knew, such as the heart symbol featured in 'I ❤ U'. In fact, Mohammed's complex 'car' text contains a variety of symbols which represent meaning in different ways. The image of the car is iconic (it resembles a car visually), the heart symbol is logographic (it stands for the idea of love) and the letter 'U' is a phonetic transcription of the word 'you'. 'Nissan' and 'Mohammed' are alphabetic. 'ABC' is alphabetic of course, but it is also a letter string which children use to stand for the alphabet itself – so 'ABC' is an icon which means 'writing'. The 'car' text shows how Mohammed was exploring the potential of literacy in a great variety of ways.

An understanding of Mohammed's varied approach to literacy helped us to interpret the texts he made in the nursery and to appreciate the value of each one. Mohammed's recipe and order form may look quite different from his alphabet poster and car text – in fact, an adult might think they were done by a different child, someone still not able to write alphabetically or who did not want to do so. But it was Mohammed who produced all of these texts – a child who enjoyed exploring alphabets and was already able to write detailed letters in both English and Arabic. In his recipe and his order form, he chose to use other kinds of representation.

Gunther Kress (1997) has suggested that young children make 'motivated choices' when designing a text, focusing on the ways in which they can best express the message they wish to convey. Sometimes this is through drawing or painting or writing, or a combination of these, or using different kinds of media. Kate Pahl (1999) shows how children experiment with these ways of making meaning in a nursery setting. The multilingual environment of Mohammed's nursery class afforded him a pool of resources including visuals, logos, and symbols from different languages, on which he drew to make texts which suited his particular purposes. As he did so, he could think through and develop his ideas as an emerging multilingual writer.

**85**

## Ideas for developing children's knowledge of symbols and text design

- To find out whether children are learning about other writing systems as well as English, you can ask if they or their siblings attend community language classes after school or at the weekends. Do they see siblings doing homework from the classes? Can they bring you any materials to show what they are learning? Are parents showing them written models of the language?

- You can encourage children to bring into the classroom any writing and images they find interesting – in leaflets, magazines, books, cereal packets, video sleeves – and talk together about what these symbols stand for.

- Teachers can look out for the particular symbols which each child is currently using in their emergent writing. Parents can help to interpret these, since they know about their children's enthusiasms and their recent participation in literacy events. For example, Mohammed's mother helped us to understand why he was drawing images of cars and writing 'M O T' and 'I ❤ U' in the nursery.

- A wide range of texts can be provided in the classroom for children to use as a resource when writing. On the bookshelves, in the home corner and on the walls children will then be surrounded by pictures, diagrams, maps, logos and writing from different languages. This will encourage them to experiment with a range of possibilities for text design.

- You can welcome children's efforts to combine different types of symbol when making texts. For example, bilingual and monolingual children may start to use writing from different languages. You can talk with the young writers about what these symbols mean and why they decided to use them.

- You may find that children are concentrating on different aspects of text design at different moments. For example, sometimes their focus may be on visual images (like Mohammed's recipe) while at other times it might be on the details of the writing (like his alphabet poster). Ask them to tell you more about what they have focused on.

- When looking at texts with children – from storybooks to the class register, from the school newsletter to home corner 'cafe menus' – you can explore questions such as:

    How are visuals and writing arranged on the page and why has this layout been chosen?

    What ideas are being illustrated by the pictures or diagrams?

    Does the writing say the same thing as the visuals or does it say something different?

    If the writing and visuals say different things, why is the child using images to show some ideas and words to show others?

This explicit discussion will help children to think through their ideas about what symbols mean, and about ways of designing texts. It can be included as part of whole class work in the Literacy Hour.

# Conclusion

'Home pages' begin as part of children's everyday literacy experience: the Turkish newspapers read by Recep's family, the Arabic alphabet chart studied by Mohammed and his mother, the Indian film videos watched by Meera's family, the airletters Billy's mother wrote to Thailand with Billy sitting beside her. When these materials are brought into school, they represent children's 'literacy worlds' and help to make the classroom into a familiar setting.

At school, new 'home pages' can be produced for the purposes of literacy learning. Parents, children and teachers can work together to build on the understandings gained from home. Recep, helped by his mother and his aunt, made his own newspapers. He combined newspaper cuttings with his knowledge of Turkish culture acquired from satellite TV and included experiences that were part of his personal life. Mohammed used his mother's Arabic alphabet poster as a basis for making his own complete and detailed alphabet in the nursery. This gave him the opportunity to write in Arabic and to add to the reading work he was already doing at home. Over three months, Meera produced five versions of her mother's video poster, each of which gave her new insights into Gujarati and English literacy. Billy wrote his own airletter sitting beside his mother in the nursery and this inspired him to do a great deal of further writing both at home and school, in English and in Thai.

Future 'home pages' will allow children to use the resources of electronic media to represent themselves and their worlds on a computer screen. The purpose of a 'home page' on the web is to present information about the person or people who set it up and make links internationally with other internet users. This opens up exciting possibilities for bilingual children to write fully about their lives and ideas and to engage in dialogue with others in a multilingual world.

Electronic 'home pages' will be multimodal, making use of visuals, sound and action to convey meaning. Young children are accustomed to reading texts of this kind and are open to ways of creating them – probably more so than many adults whose literacy experience is based in a pre-electronic age. Mohammed's awareness of different kinds of graphic symbol and his readiness to combine images with writing shows us the way forward. At the age of 4, Mohammed could discriminate between three script systems and write in two of them. He was also intrigued by logos such as the 'heart' symbol and acronyms such as 'MOT', and made use of them in his texts. He understood the power of visuals and chose to represent concepts through images as well as writing.

As educators, are we helping children to develop their capacities as makers of multilingual and multimodal texts? Government policy currently emphasises the importance of education in maximising options for the future, and we need to ensure that bilingual children's options are thoroughly recognised and included. At any time in the future these young people may decide that they want to make use of biliteracy for work or study. Rather than closing the doors to bilingual learning as soon as they enter school, the education system has a responsibility to keep the doors open for them to do so.

Young children entering the school system are ready to make use of their entire range of language resources for learning. In doing so, they can build multilingual and multicultural identities that will give them a position of strength from which to approach the future. Meera's making of the Gujarati wordsearch containing the names of her English football team exemplifies how ready children are to combine aspects of their cultural and linguistic experience in a flexible and creative way. It is up to us to give them the chance, by offering a curriculum which integrates children's 'literacy worlds'.

88

The research discussed in this book indicates that the gap often existing between home and school, particularly for bilingual children, can be bridged. But this cannot be done by a one-way flow of ideas and information from school to home. Texts and talk need also to come from home to school, as parents share with teachers their knowledge about children's daily lives and the reading and writing practices which interest them. Two-way traffic will yield much greater rewards, enabling all the adults concerned to build up their understanding of children's educational development. The children, meanwhile, will be able to draw upon and develop the full range of their literacy resources both at home and at school. And this will give bilingual children an excellent start in the early years of their education.

# References and further reading

Baker, C. (1995) *A parents' and teachers' guide to bilingualism*. Clevedon: Multilingual Matters

Baker, C. (1996) *Foundations of bilingual education and bilingualism*. Clevedon: Multilingual Matters

Chana, U., Edwards, V. and Walker, S. (1997) Calligrapher or keyboard operator? Multilingual word processing in the primary school. *Multicultural Teaching*, 16, 1

Cummins, J. (1984) *Bilingualism and special education: issues in assessment and pedagogy*. Clevedon: Multilingual Matters

Cummins, J. (1991) Interdependence of first and second language proficiency in bilingual children. In Bialystok, E. (ed) *Language processing in bilingual children*. Cambridge: Cambridge University Press

Cummins, J. (1996) *Negotiating identities: education for empowerment in a diverse society*. Ontario, California: California Association for Bilingual Education, and Stoke-on-Trent: Trentham Books

DfEE (1998) *The National Literacy Strategy*. Annesley, Notts.: DfEE Publications

Edwards, V. (1995) *Writing in multilingual classrooms*. Reading: Reading and Language Information Centre, University of Reading

Edwards, V. (1996) *The other languages: a guide to multilingual classrooms*. Reading: Reading and Language Information Centre, Reading University

Edwards, V. (1998) *The power of Babel: teaching and learning in multilingual classrooms*. Stoke-on-Trent: Trentham Books

European Commission (1996) *Accomplishing Europe through education and training*. Brussels: European Commission DGXXII

Gravelle, M. (1996) *Supporting bilingual learners in schools*. Stoke-on-Trent: Trentham Books

Green, P. (1999) *Raise the Standard*. Stoke-on-Trent: Trentham Books

Gregory, E. (1993) Reading between the lines. *Times Educational Supplement,* October 15

Gregory, E. (1996) *Making sense of a new world: learning to read in a second language*. London: Paul Chapman

Gregory, E. (ed) (1997) *One child, many worlds: early learning in multicultural communities*. London: David Fulton

Hall, N. and Robinson, A. (1995) *Exploring writing and play in the early years*. London: David Fulton

Heath, S.B. (1983) *Ways with words*. Cambridge: Cambridge University Press

Houlton, D. (1985) *All our languages*. London: Hodder & Stoughton

Kenner, C. (1997) A child writes from her everyday world: using home texts to develop biliteracy at school. In Gregory, E. (ed). *op.cit.*

Kress, G. (1997) *Before writing: rethinking the paths to literacy*. London: Routledge

McWilliam, N. (1998) *What's in a word? Vocabulary development in multilingual classrooms*. Stoke-on-Trent: Trentham Books

Martin-Jones, M. and Bhatt, A. (1999) Literacies in the lives of bilingual learners in local communities in Britain. In South, H. (ed) *Literacies in community and school.* Watford: National Association for Language Development in the Curriculum (Available from NALDIC, South Herts EMA Centre, Holywell School site, Watford WD1 8NT)

Multilingual Resources for Children Project (1995) *Building bridges: multilingual resources for children.* Clevedon: Multilingual Matters

National Writing Project (1990) *A rich resource: writing and language diversity.* Walton-on-Thames: Nelson

Pahl, K. (1999) *Transformations: meaning making in nursery education.* Stoke-on-Trent: Trentham Books

Rashid, N. and Gregory, E. (1997) Learning to read, reading to learn: the importance of siblings in the language development of young bilingual children. In Gregory, E. (ed). *op.cit.*

Ramirez, J.D. (1992) Longitudinal study of structured English immersion strategy, early-exit and late-exit transitional bilingual programs for language minority children. *Bilingual Research Journal,* 16

Saxena, M. (1994) Literacies among Panjabis in Southall. In Hamilton, M., Barton, D. and Ivanic, R. (eds) *Worlds of Literacy.* Clevedon: Multilingual Matters

Sneddon, R. (1993) Beyond the National Curriculum: a community project to support bilingualism. *Journal of Multilingual and Multicultural Development,* 4, 3

Street, B. (1984) *Literacy in theory and practice.* Cambridge: CUP

Taylor, D. (1983) *Family literacy: young children learning to read and write.* London: Heinemann

Taylor, D. and Dorsey-Gaines, C. (1988) *Growing up literate.* London: Heinemann Educational

Thomas, W. and Collier, V. (1997) *School effectiveness and language minority students.* Washington DC: National Clearinghouse for Bilingual Education

Welsh Language Board (1999) *Two languages: twice the choice.* Cardiff: Welsh Language Board

Welsh Language Board (1999) *Raising bilingual children: a resource pack for health professionals.* Cardiff: Welsh Language Board

# INDEX

92